Praise for *Decluttering at the Speed of Life*

"This book is another home run for Dana. For the past ten-plus years, I have been a stay-at-home scatterbrained dad. My wife has been the main source of income, and I assumed I would never get this home stuff figured out. It wasn't until I did a Google search with the words *slob* and *clean* that I found the help I needed. When I saw the word *deslobification*, I knew I was at the right place.

"Dana is the GPS of housecleaning and decluttering. No matter how far you have strayed on your journey trying to get your home in order, she has a path to get you back on track. . . . If you're looking for a book on decluttering that makes sense, this is for you."
—WILLIAM B., GREENVILLE, SOUTH CAROLINA
DAD OF THREE

"Dana shares a real, practical, step-by-step process for getting rid of the stuff, and she does it with humor and plenty of grace for the messiness and difficulties of life. The section on helping kids declutter is especially useful!"
—JEAN P., CHICO, CALIFORNIA
MOM OF TWO, LIBRARIAN, SEAMSTRESS

"Dana gets it. I've spent my entire life feeling like something was wrong with me. I excelled in school and at work, so why couldn't I handle my house? I never knew anyone else had ever been reduced to tears over the state of their home. When my husband suddenly passed away, amidst my grief, I could no longer cope with the clutter. I started by doing the dishes, and gradually worked my way up to decluttering my entire home, trash and easy stuff first.

"Dana handles the issue of decluttering dreams with sensitivity. I may not be ready to part with all, or even most, of my late husband's things, but my house is so much better. And better is wonderful!"
—KIM H., GREEN BROOK, NEW JERSEY
WIDOWED MOM OF TWO

"The phrase *game changer* may be cliché, but it's true. This book is hard to put down yet makes you want to roll up your sleeves and start decluttering. I'd also refer to it as I tackled each room. It has valuable lessons about what five minutes can do and how to evaluate your mess in easy steps. I found it relatable as to how clutter causes stress and how much happier I could be to let go and 'live in the now.' Dana is a kind voice telling you you're not alone, and she helps you tap into the potential you have to get started."

—SUSAN L., NORTHBRIDGE, MASSACHUSETTS
RECENTLY DIVORCED WOMAN WHO MOVED 3000 SQUARE
FEET OF BELONGINGS TO A 730-SQUARE-FOOT HOME

"I've found a kindred spirit in Dana. She gets me! She thinks like me and struggles like me. Dana guides you in an ever-so-gentle way to get on top of your clutter. I appreciated her encouragement, which was nonjudgmental and motivating at the same time. I was entertained by her humor and inspired by her simple approach. The state of my home is improving incrementally by the day. Thank you for giving me hope and the tools to move toward normalcy."

—AILIM H., SYDNEY, AUSTRALIA
FULL-TIME WORKING MOTHER OF A TODDLER

"Dana White hits a perfect 'best friend/girls' night out' balance between real talk and humor in *Decluttering at the Speed of Life*. Her upbeat and engaging writing sets out clear steps to declutter your home and reframe your mind-set. As a Manhattan professional and mother, I have to make sure that to the outside world my life seems pulled together. My big secret and biggest struggle has been my ongoing fight with clutter. As the child of a hoarder, I always knew I wanted a cleaner home, but all the books on organizing didn't help me. *Decluttering at the Speed of Life* is different. Dana is really clear about what the book can and can't do. She gives simple frameworks for how to get started, stay motivated, and get back on track after a relapse. Since working with Dana's frameworks, I can make my unpredictable schedule still work for our household. The chaos is calmed—and we have even been able to have guests over for the first time!"

—MADDY, NEW YORK, NEW YORK
ASSISTANT PRINCIPAL AND MOM

"Dana White provides stressed-out homemakers with a simple declutter-ing method that works. In writing laced with humor, charm, and wisdom, Dana shares from personal experience how to go about dealing with this monstrosity, the insides of our homes. Using the five easy steps, I tackled the worst room in my house and was so pleased with the results. Life is crazy busy, and clutter and mess is inevitable, but by implementing Dana's clear-cut approach, one can achieve an orderly, tranquil sanctuary."

—JOANNE G., HALIFAX, NOVA SCOTIA
WIFE, MOTHER, AND HOMEMAKER

"This book is not like any other cleaning, organizing, or self-help book. It's real and genuine. The only problem I had was that I wanted to both get up and declutter and keep reading it at the same time. Truly inspiring and entirely original."

—CYNDI L., SALEM, OREGON
WORKING, HOMESCHOOLING, VOLUNTEERING MOM

"How do you eat an elephant? One bite at a time. How can I declutter my home? One room at a time. Dana has broken down this seemingly monu-mental task room by room and step by step to get the most impact for my efforts and to keep the ball rolling. Whether I have a few minutes, a few hours, a few days, or more, Dana's methods (and humor) motivate and ener-gize me to jump in and tackle one space at a time instead of drowning at the enormity of it all. Just following her steps for one room in my home imme-diately made me feel better being in that space and made me want more (of that feeling, not more stuff—definitely not more stuff!). Decluttering at the speed of life means doing what you can, when you can, and celebrating those victories with Dana cheering you on from the stands."

—TAMMY M., PHOENIX, ARIZONA
PROFESSIONAL FULL-TIME WORKING MOM OF TWO BOYS

Decluttering
AT THE
Speed of Life

Also by Dana K. White

*How to Manage Your Home
Without Losing Your Mind*

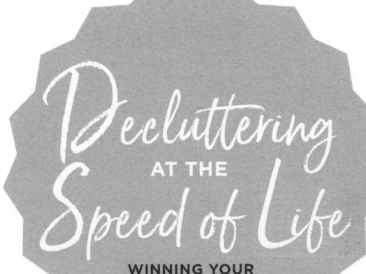

Decluttering

AT THE

Speed of Life

WINNING YOUR
NEVER-ENDING BATTLE
WITH STUFF

DANA K. WHITE

W PUBLISHING GROUP

AN IMPRINT OF THOMAS NELSON

Published in Nashville, Tennessee, by W Publishing, an imprint of Thomas Nelson.

Thomas Nelson titles may be purchased in bulk for educational, business, fund-raising, or sales promotional use. For information, please e-mail SpecialMarkets@ ThomasNelson.com.

Any Internet addresses, phone numbers, or company or product information printed in this book are offered as a resource and are not intended in any way to be or to imply an endorsement by Thomas Nelson, nor does Thomas Nelson vouch for the existence, content, or services of these sites, phone numbers, companies, or products beyond the life of this book.

ISBN 978-0-7180-8060-0 (SC)
ISBN 978-0-7180-8358-8 (e-book)

Library of Congress Cataloging-in-Publication Data
Library of Congress Control Number: 2017917449

Printed in the United Kingdom
23   CPI   52

To all those willing to say, "Me too!"
Knowing I wasn't the only one who struggled
with clutter freed me to do whatever it
took to solve this crazy problem.

Contents

Contents

PART 2: DECLUTTERING ROOM BY ROOM

PART 3: HELPING OTHERS DECLUTTER

PART 4: SPECIAL CIRCUMSTANCES IN DECLUTTERING

DECLUTTERING EXPERT?

Hello. My name is Dana, and I am a Decluttering Expert.

That sentence makes me laugh. And cringe.

I suffer from excessive honesty, so it took me a very (*very*) long time to call myself a Decluttering Expert. I never imagined I could be or would want to be one. But I am.

I'm a Decluttering Expert because I have decluttered. I have purged my home of literal truckloads of junk. I have opened random doors and slammed them shut, feeling completely and totally overwhelmed, and then opened them again and worked my way through the clutter inside.

I've dealt with my own stuff. My own sentimental attachments. My own excessive need to be prepared for any and every scenario that could possibly happen between now and the day my great-great-grandchildren die.

I've collected the supplies needed to live my ideal life and then pried those supplies from my own tight grip as I adjusted to the reality of the life I'm actually living.

I've learned how to get rid of things even though I wanted to keep them all. I've learned to like living my life with only things that make it better. I've consciously decided to view my home as a place to live instead of a place to store all my great ideas and their attached stuff. I've done all that even though it was completely unnatural to me.

I've had to come up with real-life ways to break through real-life clutter in my own real life.

And much to my surprise, along the way the strategies I put into words helped other people declutter their stuff.

So after years of asking that no one look to me for decluttering advice or inspiration or instruction, I gave up, gave in, and accepted this role of Decluttering Guru to the People of the Internet.

But before I share with you my hard-learned wisdom, let's get a few things straight.

THINGS TO KNOW BEFORE YOU READ

There are some things you need to understand before you get into the meat of this book. I'm one person, and the strategies I share are the ones that continue to work for me and make a lasting impact in my home. There will be moments when you love what I say, and there will be moments when you hate my guts.

This book shall contain no complicated systems, pretty photos, detailed charts or graphs, or even checklists. The goal here is to get stuff out of the house. And that's it. And that is enough.

This book is for the person who is ready to declutter. I wrote it to help you purge your own stuff from your own home. I didn't write it to help you change someone else who you wish would declutter. I will talk about helping others declutter, but it's still about you and what you can do. You can only change you, and understanding that fact now will prevent a whole lot of heartache in your future.

I won't solve your personal problems. I don't know the ins and outs of every detail of the unique challenges you face. I don't know your physical disability or your town's garbage policies or what causes you to hold tight to certain categories of clutter or the details of your exhausting work schedule.

But I do know this: these strategies work, and they are boiled down to the very basics so they work in any home for people in any situation. I know because they work for me and for people with lives very different from mine.

I will address (some of) your unique delusions. Certain things I say might make you mad. I know this because I despised facing my own reality at one time. Letting go of my own excuses was harder than getting up and decluttering. Just thought you should know.

I won't judge you. We'll celebrate any progress you make, whether large or small.

Following the steps in this book won't be dramatic. We won't be emptying any rooms or creating any cutesy organizing systems worthy of a magazine. There aren't any pictures to flip through and make you feel inspired, dreaming of how your house could be.

But you will make progress every time you follow the steps (or even one step) to working through an overwhelming mess. People used to seeing your mess will start wondering what is happening, why the house feels bigger and is staying under control more easily and for longer periods of time. Change will happen, but it won't necessarily involve big reveals.

I'll step on all kinds of idealistic toes. My goal in this book is to help you declutter. To help you get things out of your house. I'm going to default to the words *trash* and *donate* even though that may get your undies in a wad every single time.

When I say *trash*, you're smart enough to know I mean your recycling bin if you have one. But for some people who live in areas without access to recycling, guilt over not being able to recycle is paralyzing, and *technically recyclable* stuff builds up in their homes. So I'll say *trash*. *Trash*: things going *either* to the dump *or* to a recycling center.

I'm also going to use the word *donate*. If you want to sell things, sell things. *As long as you actually sell them.* I have an entire chapter about how deciding to donate instead of selling significantly accelerated my decluttering progress.

Some data is real, but most is experiential. All strategies are based on my personal experiences, but sometimes I quote a number. Unless I specifically say where I got that number, I probably made it up.

I like to make up statistics and percentages and decimals. Usually, these made-up numbers serve the purpose of showing how likely I am to do or not do something. If you're a mathematician, I apologize. I taught theatre arts, so numbers mostly serve as dramatic effect for me.

I'll talk about the steps to working through an overwhelming mess again and again (and again). I've created specific steps to help me break through that all-too-familiar feeling of being *totally* overwhelmed by clutter. Those steps work in any space and for any clutter level, and a big chunk of the book will be applying those steps to specific areas of your house. You'll have the steps memorized by the end of the book, but that's pretty much the point.

You might need to read this book more than once. Life happens, and it brings clutter along for the ride. As long as you're living, there will be new stuff coming in and old stuff that needs to leave. And that's fine. Accepting this universal truth took me far in my own decluttering journey.

Feel free to take some strategies and leave others. Do what you want to do. There's no wrong way to declutter. As long as stuff you don't need leaves your home, you're doing awesome.

If you read my first book, you'll recognize some of the concepts in this book. I have no interest in reinventing any wheels, and I only share what works, but this time we're going deep. We'll work through your home, step by step, and address unique challenges that pop up in each area.

I know some of you will skip ahead to the how-do-I-fix-my-house-right-now section. That's fine. But know that the mind-set changes I address in the beginning of this book are crucial to lasting change in your home.

This is going to be fun. Not the decluttering, but the reading.

PART 1

Building a Decluttering Mind-Set

Chapter 1

WHAT DECLUTTERING IS AND ISN'T

Decluttering is stuff you don't need leaving your house. And that's really all it is. If five things leave or five hundred things leave, you've succeeded.

Decluttering isn't Stuff Shifting. It isn't rearranging or buying a new shelving unit or sorting into slots or drawers or baskets.

Decluttering isn't organizing. When I realized decluttering and organizing were two different things and that it was okay to *just* declutter, I felt a weight lift off my soul. I no longer slumped my shoulders in defeat before I even started, knowing from experience that whatever "solution" I might create would surely fail like all the others had. Instead, I purged. I focused solely on getting things we didn't need out of our house.

When I did that, a weight lifted off my home as well. As things left, life was easier, and my home functioned better than it had after any of my attempts at organizing, just because there was *less*. Eventually, I understood that is what decluttering actually is: achieving *less*.

But before we jump in, I want to go over some key terms. Through my own decluttering escapades I've come up with ways of explaining things to myself. Those of you who already know me and my made-up decluttering language will nod along. But if you are new to my style of decluttering, don't get overwhelmed. We're going to apply these concepts to each area of your home. If anything makes you say, "Wha . . . ? I don't get that . . ." I promise you'll get it as you read the book. We'll go step by step through your home and your hang-ups.

My favorite made-up word is *deslobification*. It's what I call the process through which I improved my own home from a constant state of *oh-my-word-what-is-wrong-with-me* to *I-can-totally-do-this-even-though-it's-never-going-to-be-perfect*. Going from a worse-than-bad home to a livable one is how I learned these strategies and principles, and how I found a way to translate concepts that other people seemed to be born knowing into words that make sense to me and a lot of other people.

I definitely didn't make up the word *clutter*, but I did make up a definition for it that helped me get it out of my house. I define *clutter* as anything I can't keep under control. If a space in my home consistently gets out of control, I have too much stuff in that space. I have clutter.

Once I defined clutter this way, I finally understood why my friend and I can buy the same décor, and her house looks like a magazine but mine looks like a thrift store. I have a *Clutter Threshold*, and it's unique to me. My Clutter Threshold is the point at which stuff becomes clutter in my home. When I'm living above my Clutter Threshold, there's more stuff in my home than I can handle, and my house is consistently out of control. Living under my Clutter Threshold helps my home stay more naturally under control. I found mine (and you'll find yours) through decluttering.

But it wasn't easy. I suffered from *Decluttering Paralysis*, a real phenomenon that makes me unable to move when facing an overwhelming mess. I cured it by moving. By starting with the easy stuff. And strangely, every time I did something easy, the space looked better, and I was less overwhelmed.

Not that I don't make mistakes. I totally do. But I've accepted that while *Decluttering Regret* (the realization that I need something *after* I declutter it) isn't fun, I've survived every time. And the peace I feel over a home that's easier to manage outweighs the frustration I feel over having to write "medium-sized cutting board" on my shopping list. I accepted that people with homes that are consistently under control prefer living with regret over living with clutter. I want to be one of those people.

But even though Decluttering Paralysis and Decluttering Regret are terms that make me sigh, this one gives me hope: *Decluttering Momentum*. It's a real phenomenon. By starting with easy stuff and working through the steps I'm sharing in this book, I saw visible, measurable improvement in my home. As my home changed, I changed. And decluttering got easier and easier. I'm so excited for you to experience that too.

MY CLUTTER HISTORY

I had to develop decluttering strategies out of necessity. I couldn't go on living the way I'd been living, with stuff (quite literally) spilling out of every cabinet door, covering every surface, and taking up every last available space in my home.

I had to dig my way out, and it was the most unnatural thing I'd ever done. If I'm left to my natural tendencies, clutter builds, and clutter stays.

I didn't know it was clutter. I thought it was all amazingly useful stuff. I just needed a moment to remember why I'd considered it useful in the moment I brought it through my front (or side or back) door.

And that totally logical thinking was how I ended up in a place where I couldn't function in my own home. I couldn't even use my second largest room, and the rooms I could use were difficult to use because I had to work around all sorts of extra and unnecessary things, even though I didn't realize they were extra and unnecessary.

You want proof I know what it's like to deal with clutter?

When my husband and I got married, he was thirty-two and I was twenty-five. We'd each lived alone and had whatever we needed to live alone.

Our marriage meant moving into one apartment that was, honestly, pretty large for a newly married couple just starting out. If I remember correctly, it was 960 square feet.

In that 960 square feet we had three dining tables. One formal dining table was in the dining area. Another formal dining table was awkwardly shoved in the teeny-tiny breakfast nook. And the small table (the one that actually made sense for a newlywed couple to have) was in the room we used for storage. The room that had boxes piled to the ceiling.

Eighteen years later I see the ridiculousness of our table situation, but at the time it didn't seem even a little bit strange. The apartment wasn't our "real" house. It was temporary. Who knew what kind of home or dining-area situation our future would bring? Why in the world *wouldn't* I keep all three tables until we knew what we needed in our real house? We were ready for the future and *all* the possibilities it could *possibly* bring.

Even the dining area (that fit one of the full-sized formal dining tables) was cramped. The walls were stacked waist high (at least) with more storage boxes full of totally-useful-in-the-future stuff. Or at least I assumed they were full of useful-in-the-future stuff. I didn't remember what was inside them.

Then we moved, and the house we moved into was a *real* house.

As we left that first apartment, my parents hired professional movers as a gift to us. I was about four months pregnant with our first child, and I appreciated their thoughtfulness so much. Those movers had no idea what they were getting into when they agreed to pack up and move our stuff. One of the men spent the entire day in my kitchen. My teeny-tiny kitchen in the apartment where exactly zero formal dinner parties had been held. All day. *Just packing dishes.*

We moved into our 1,752-square-foot real home from the 960-square-foot apartment and purged huge amounts of excess that we'd never needed. And we still ended up with more stuff than space.

And then I became a stay-at-home mom. As we adjusted to living on a single income, I discovered garage sales and fell head over heels in love with them. I'd been to garage sales before, but I became obsessed. I loved having a way to go shopping for pennies, since pennies were all we could afford to spend on nonnecessities.

With the you-never-know-what-you'll-find excitement of garage sales and the might-as-well-keep-it-if-there's-any-chance-I-might-use-it-one-day mentality I already had, our already cluttered home grew more and more cluttered.

When we moved again, and it was time to pack up our 1,752-square-foot house, I reserved the biggest moving truck I could find, which the rental place said could fit the contents of a typical 3,000-square-foot home. We filled that truck completely—and still left behind our entire master bedroom suite, our dining set, a full-sized couch, various other furniture items, and many more boxes of stuff.

We had enough to furnish a rental house *and* make the house we were selling look livable.

Once that house sold, we rented another moving truck (this time for a 2,000-square-foot house) *and* filled up our minivan *and* my mother's minivan. We brought *all that stuff* to our 1,400-square-foot rental house. For a year, we lived with *all that stuff* in that house. The two-car garage was completely full of boxes, and boxes lined every wall of our living area.

But never once did I consider getting rid of the boxes that were making our everyday life difficult. I needed that stuff for the future. Or I *might* need it for the future.

It was not that I didn't know I needed to declutter. At the end of our time in our first real house and through our transition year, I started selling on eBay with the exact purpose of getting rid of stuff. Purging was my goal. But I almost immediately started *buying* things at garage sales so I could sell them on eBay. My purpose shifted from getting rid of stuff to making money.

It wasn't a slippery slope. It was a landslide. A landslide so fast and violent that my most adamant request for a new home was that it have an eBay room.

You're right; I should have known. Looking at the past, I can see my severely flawed thought processes, but at the time I couldn't.

I did not understand that my overabundance of stuff was directly related to my inability to function well in my home. The more stuff I brought into my home, the more out of control it felt. The more out of control my home felt, the more I looked to the future as the time when I'd finally have things figured out. The more I focused on the future instead of the present, the more I justified collecting things I might need one day.

> **Living for now became my new goal: living in the house we have, in the city where we are, and in the moment when we're alive.**

The cycle continued and increased in force, and I felt increasingly out of control. This ultimately swirled me straight into a place called *rock bottom*. Rock bottom happened in the home where I live now.

At rock bottom, I stopped bringing stuff in and started getting stuff out. As I got stuff out of my house, living in it became easier. As living in my house became easier, I liked my house more. I didn't have as much stuff tripping me, blocking my path, and falling out of cabinets on top of me.

And that was when I made a conscious choice to live in the phase of life I was in. Right then. I decided to stop assuming I knew what I'd love to already have in the future.

Living for now became my new goal: living in the house we have, in the city where we are, and in the moment when we're alive.

This doesn't mean forgetting the future exists. Living now means giving *now* preferential treatment over the future or even the past.

Living now means I need a dining table that is consistently (or at least easily) clear of stuff. I am passionate about eating together as a family around the dinner table. It's one of my core values, and it needs to happen now. If I put that off, my kids will be gone, and the opportunity will be gone as well.

There's a constant rotation of dishes and newspapers and school projects going onto and off of our table, but that table can't be the permanent resting place of anything that doesn't directly contribute to eating dinner as a family. Cute vase, napkin holder, and a salt and pepper set? Great. Printer, paper shredder, and jewelry tree? Nope.

Living now means my kids can easily get dressed for school because the only things in their drawers and closets are clothes that fit. Not clothes they outgrew two years ago or clothes they'll grow into someday.

Living now means open floor space so my sons can wrestle. It means I can walk to my bathroom in the middle of the night without stubbing a toe. It means my daughter has space to dance around in her room.

I know these things are obvious, and I would have said they were obvious to me too. But I wasn't *living* like they were obvious.

I'm telling you my story because I know how hard it is to completely change your thinking about stuff. I also know how hard it is to take advice from someone who doesn't understand. I have stood in my own home, completely overwhelmed, crying tears of frustration and hopelessness over my inability to deal with the sheer volume of clutter.

I have trialed and I have errored and I have succeeded. I've used every imaginable way to get stuff out of my house, and I know what works and what doesn't. I've experienced the joy of an after photo and the agony of another disaster reappearing in that same space. And I've decluttered again.

You can totally do this. I did.

Chapter 3

ACCEPTING THAT YOUR HOUSE IS A CONTAINER

T he single biggest mind-set change, the greatest moment of under-standing, the most impactful I-can-let-go-of-my-stuff pivot in my cluttered home didn't come from hearing an inspirational speech or experiencing an emotional trauma.

Honestly, it wasn't emotional at all, and I believe that's why the moment had such an impact on me. I finally understood what I now call the *Container Concept*.

The basic idea is this: the purpose of a container is to contain.

According to Dictionary.com, *contain* has multiple definitions. These are the ones that speak to my clutter-collecting soul:

to keep under proper control;
to prevent or limit the expansion, influence, success, or advance of;
to succeed in preventing the spread of[1]

Those definitions describe what I was desperate to make happen in my home. Keep things under proper control? Mm-hmm. Prevent or

---

1. *Dictionary.com Unabridged*, s. v. "contain," Random House, Inc., accessed July 5, 2017, http://www.dictionary.com/browse/contain.

limit the expansion or advance of my stuff? Yeah, baby. Succeed in preventing the spread of clutter? Yes, please!

But I kept buying containers, filling them up, and buying more. And my house was worse off every time I did. I was using those containers incorrectly because *I didn't understand their purpose.*

Used properly, containers are limits. They keep clutter from spreading. They keep stuff under proper control by preventing *and* limiting the expansion of that stuff. But how?

I thought the purpose of containers was to hold stuff. That's why I kept buying more when the ones I had were full and I still had stuff that needed to be held.

I assumed there was a solution lurking just beyond my current organizing abilities. Someday, when I reached that elusive State of Organization, my stuff would all work together perfectly, and I'd be glad to have whatever I already had.

But as long as I was using containers incorrectly, I was never going to reach that State of Organization.

I'm going to choose an example that will surely offend some but could be neutral and nonemotional for others. If you're offended, please replace the word *scarf* with something that doesn't upset you to consider decluttering. You can replace it with any item in your entire house, because the Container Concept applies to everything: forks, shoes, cans of black beans, or books. (Yes, I just said *books*.)

Scarves are accessories. They dress up or change the look of an outfit. They're useful. I can't personally wear them, because I have issues with things being wrapped around my neck, but some people love them. Like, they love them so much they have walls and closets full of scarves.

At first glance, there seems to be no reason to even think about how many scarves you have. Scarves are small. They can be hung or folded or dropped carelessly into a box with other scarves.

Before I understood the Container Concept, decluttering scarves would have gone like this:

Ugh. My closet floor is covered in scarves. I know it's not possible to have too many scarves, because scarves are useful and having choices is essential to fashionable living, but I'm really tired of my closet floor being covered in scarves.

I know what I'll do! I'll use one of those five different scarf-organizing systems I've purchased over the past few years! I need to get organized!

Oh, wow! This hanging-on-the-wall system is awesome! That looks fabulous! I am the best . . . ugh. My floor is still *covered in scarves.*

Mm-kay. I'll use the scarf hangers my mom bought me after the last time she looked in my closet.

Yes! Scarf hangers full! Go me . . . blergh. How is my floor still covered in scarves?! Now *what do I do?*

Here's exactly what I'd have done before I understood the Container Concept: bought more wall-hanging-organizing thingies and more scarf hangers until the floor was clear but there was no more wall space because it was covered in wall-hanging-organizing thingies and no more room for my clothes because the closet rods were full of scarf hangers.

And when one of those wall thingies fell (because even though scarves are feather-light, I'd shoved six too many on it), the only thing I knew to do was sit on the floor of my closet and cry. And wonder why scarf organizing was so hard for me. And why my closet looked absolutely nothing like the closets in the picture on the package of wall-hanging-organizing thingies.

I might have tried to do some math. Multiply the number of days in a month with scarf-appropriate weather by some other number that entered my unnecessarily analytical brain. I might have researched scarf trends and color palettes and tried to determine which scarves were on their way out of style.

I'd hold each scarf up, maybe try it on, and analyze it for its inherent worthiness. I might even research which colors look best with my skin tone. I might close my eyes, take a deep breath, and try to recall how I felt the last time I wore each one.

And all that time, all that thinking, all that analysis would let me get rid of eight to ten scarves—not even enough to make a visible dent in the piles.

But once I understood the purpose of containers, I was freed from my overthinking. Once I understood that the purpose of a container is to contain, I saw that though the container *held* the scarves, its most important purpose was to *limit* the number of scarves I kept. Once the scarf container was full, I knew how many scarves I could keep.

The kind of container isn't the issue. Anything can be a container: a wall-hanging thingy, a scarf hanger, a few nails in the wall, a drawer in your dresser, a basket, a shelf, whatever. Any defined space that holds scarves is the scarf container.

How does it work?

- Fill the container with your favorite scarves first.
- Once the container is full, you know how many scarves you can keep.
- Donate the rest of the scarves.

Accept the limitations of the space you have, and declutter enough that your stuff fits comfortably in that space.

You can keep as many scarves as will comfortably fit in the space you have available for scarves. If you would look for scarves in your closet, the space you have available for scarves depends on the size of your closet and on what else you need to keep in that space.

Let's assume for the purpose of this illustration that you keep all your clothes in the closet. It's the *only* place where you keep clothes. You cannot fill the entire closet with scarves unless you are willing to wrap them around your waist for skirts, around your torso for tops, and around your feet for socks. And I suppose you'd need to tie one like a diaper for undies.

That's completely unrealistic, right? Well, contrary to what I believed, so is thinking there's no limit to how many scarves I can keep.

If a closet needs to hold all your clothing, the size of that closet determines how many clothes you can have. It's a limit.

And if you have more clothing than will fit in the closet, you have clothing outside that closet. Clothing with no home because its home is already full.

And that's how the Out-of-Control Home Thing happens.

I did not see my closets or drawers or cabinets as limits, and my house was out of control. I complained that I had no room for all my stuff, but I was trying to keep more stuff than could physically fit into my home.

Once I started looking at the size of the scarf shelf as the limit to how many scarves I could keep, instead of as the pretty place (that never actually looked pretty) to shove scarves, I made progress. Immediately.

Yay for lightbulb moments.

But it got better.

I didn't decide anything. I didn't figure out anything. I just accepted that limits were limits. And accepting limits was strangely freeing.

I didn't decide anything. I didn't figure out anything. I just accepted that limits were limits. And accepting limits was strangely freeing.

Every time I felt the relief of not needing to determine the value (monetary, emotional, whatever) of something and instead asked myself whether it fit into the container I had for it, I started looking for more ways to put this drama-free strategy to work. No angst. No emotion. No analysis. I just picked out my favorites, put them in the container, and knew that when the container was full, anything left wasn't as loved as the ones in the container.

This made decluttering easy, or at least doable.

I realized that baskets and plastic shoeboxes weren't the only containers in my home. Each shelf was a container.

The size of an individual shelf determined how many baskets I could keep. The size of the cabinet determined how many shelves there were. The size of the room determined how many cabinets there were, and the size of my house determined how many rooms we had.

This may sound terribly *duh* to you, but not understanding these things had gotten me into a big mess and made our life as a family difficult. We couldn't function the way we needed to because I was ignoring the limits of our space.

This sounds crazy, I know, but it really had never occurred to me that there was a limit to how much stuff I could have in my house. I have a make-it-work personality, and I'm quick to readjust in many situations where this trait serves me well. But I also, unfortunately, readjust in situations where I shouldn't.

Since limits weren't a thing, I kept bringing more stuff into my home and kept feeling more and more overwhelmed, but I didn't understand why. I believed I needed to get organized, to find a way to fit all the stuff neatly and in a totally maintainable way.

I didn't know I was living above my Clutter Threshold. I didn't know I was exceeding both the limits of what I could handle and the space available in my home, because I didn't know there *were* limits.

I didn't know my house was a container.

I'm an includer. I like to let everyone come to everything. I'm the theatre director who is more than happy to put every person who didn't get a speaking part into the chorus so they can be a part of the production.

But this doesn't work with stuff.

The stuff I put inside my house has to fit within its limits. When I live within those limits, the house stays under control so much more easily.

I'm bossy. And a little controlling. I tried to control the capacity of my house. But the capacity of my house was determined by the person who built it, not me. Without realizing what I was doing, I was arguing with my house. I wanted to make the decisions about *my* house! *No house can tell me what to do!*

But those decisions exhausted me.

When I tried to declutter, I examined each item, attempting to assess its value to my current life, my family's current life, and our future life as a whole. I analyzed the importance of each and every item, trying to predict how much I'd use it if I kept it or how much regret I'd feel if I purged it.

Even after all that fretting, I might not have made a difference in my home. Or a difference in how we functioned.

Understanding the Container Concept fixed this completely.

When I understood that the key to successful decluttering was to purge enough stuff that I had only what fit comfortably inside the existing containers in my home (shelves, closets, and so on), no emotional decisions were necessary.

The question wasn't whether something had worth; it was whether it fit in my container. And that let me let go of things I once thought I never could.

The decision became, "Do I like this more than that?" Favorite things got first dibs at container space. Things I liked (but weren't favorites) could totally stay, guilt-free, as long as there was space. Things that didn't have a current purpose or need didn't get to stay, and I didn't even feel bad about that. There simply wasn't space.

No offense, salt-shaker-that-tends-to-clog-up—even though you would be totally useful in a pinch if we ever needed to set a third table for a big party—there's no room for you, because the two sets we use take all the space in that cabinet.

I used scarves as an example because scarves are exactly the kind of thing I'd never consider needing a limit on. But I know many of you thought some hateful thoughts about me when I mentioned books in my list of items that are subject to the Container Concept.

So let's talk about it.

Books are awesome. I read for pleasure every single day of my life. I completely understand the resistance to decluttering books.

But a bookshelf is a perfect example of a container. A bookshelf will only fit a certain number of books. Before I understood that the size of the bookshelf was the limit to how many books I could have, I shoved and I pushed and I laid books horizontally on top of the vertically placed ones after the vertical space was gone.

And I complained about how messy they looked.

Once I realized my bookshelves were containers for books, I filled them with my favorite books first, and then, once they were full, I got rid of the books that didn't fit.

That worked so much better than what I'd done before: lamenting the lack of bookshelf space and buying another bookshelf, and then lamenting the lack of space in the room for bookshelves, and then lamenting the lack of money available to buy a new home with more space for bookshelves.

That's how my brain worked before, but I had to stop the clutter. My excess stuff was ruining my ability to enjoy and function in my home.

Letting my bookshelves make the decisions for me was incredibly freeing. I stopped worrying about offending the author or giving up on the dream of turning my kids into Shakespeare lovers or admitting I'm not quite intellectual enough to choose to reread Dostoyevsky on an annual basis.

Because that's reality. It's not personal.

And I survived. Surviving freed me to bring home a new book without the sinking, guilty feeling that it might be *the* thing that makes my house implode with mess. I just had to decide which book(s) to remove so there was space for my new one. And that is the

One-In-One-Out Rule. If a container is full, and I need to put something in it, I have to remove something from the container to make room for the thing I'm putting in.

Many people are born knowing this. People like me are not.

MY FAMILY NEEDS SPACE IN
THE CONTAINER TOO

As I changed my focus from *deciding* to *fitting*, I had another moment of life-changing understanding: if my entire house is a container, my family needs to fit in that container as well.

The kitchen isn't only a holding space for pots and pans and forks; it's a space for us to live.

I need to be able to move through my kitchen without bumping into things or turning sideways. My family needs to be able to move, sit down to eat, and chop vegetables on a cutting board with plenty of open space around it for our elbows and the salad bowl.

And this helped me appreciate the purposes of the rooms in my home. I'm not willing to sacrifice my kitchen for the sake of keeping more scarves.

YOU DON'T NEED A BIGGER HOUSE

I lived in home after home, believing my problem was the size of my house.

Understanding, accepting, and implementing the Container Concept in my home changed that. I realized the house I have is the house I have.

When I stopped using living space to store things that didn't fit in the rooms where they were supposed to go, I was finally satisfied with the home I had. And I accepted that as long as I didn't live within my container, I'd overfill any house, no matter the size.

I used to have a dream (an actual, when-you're-asleep dream). Maybe you've had it too. In this dream I find rooms in my home that I hadn't known existed. I'm so, so excited they're there, and I'm relieved to learn my house is bigger than I thought it was. I'm sure there's a clutter-related psychological reason for that dream, because when I shared it on my website, others who struggle with clutter said they've had the same dream.

Once I decluttered, my house *was* bigger. With each nonpiled space I cleared, I gained usable square footage. I got the bigger house I wanted, but not by taking out a bigger mortgage. I got that house by accepting the limitations of the house I already had.

And strangely, I stopped having that dream.

VALUING SPACE OVER STUFF

I promise this chapter is about a decluttering mind-set change, but stay with me while I talk about chicken for a minute.

Comfort food is a thing, and most people know exactly what their comfort food is. For me, it's chicken fried chicken, mashed potatoes with gravy, and fried okra.

Let me clarify that I am not talking about fried chicken. Fried chicken is chicken on the bone. I like fried chicken, but I *love* chicken fried chicken. Chicken fried chicken is a boneless, skinless chicken breast that is battered and fried the way chicken fried steak is battered and fried.

I know the difference, and I find that difference to be worth a paragraph in my book about decluttering. Or worth an impassioned speech with a random person who ends up in a conversation with me and mistakenly assumes that fried chicken and chicken fried chicken are the same thing.

I also know that chicken fried chicken is my personal comfort food, and that each person defines *comfort food* differently. For some, it's pot roast. Or pork chops. Or yeast rolls. Or (and I really wish this was me) spinach smoothies. My life would be so much easier if I turned to spinach smoothies in moments of stress or sadness.

Comfort clutter is also a thing. Unfortunately, though, like comfort food, it's not usually good for me.

Comfort food tastes *so* good while I'm eating it, but the feeling doesn't last once the food is gone. This would happen with any meal, no matter how healthy. But the effects of my comfort food meal don't end there. I'm frustrated with myself for eating something that ultimately makes my life harder. Because now my jeans don't fit.

And my jeans not fitting makes me feel frustrated, and frustration makes me crave something that's been chicken fried. It's a cycle. A very bad kind of cycle.

The same thing happened when I collected stuff to satisfy the what-ifs that plague my soul. As a super-duper planner of all future possibilities, I grabbed things because I saw their potential to solve a future problem. A potential future problem. Or a potential future random idea. But the in-the-moment-of-buying feeling didn't last.

For example, a prop for a photo I might want to one day take of my child or someone else's child if I ever started a photography business. A prop like, let's say, a shoeshine box. Wouldn't it be awesome to already have a shoeshine box if I ever got inspired to dress up my kids and make them pretend to shine each other's shoes for an old-timey photo?

The chances of me feeling completely desperate over not having a shoeshine box were pretty slim, but now those chances were zero.

But when I brought a shoeshine box into my home, there was nowhere to put it, because we don't shine shoes. And I didn't have any definite plans of doing an old-timey shoe-shining photo shoot with my kids or anyone else's kids. So it went into a pile of assorted maybes.

Meanwhile, I continually complained that cleaning was hard because I didn't have places to put things away.

Except that *things* included things like shoeshine boxes.

And just as the temporary pleasure of chicken fried chicken turns into frustration and regret when my jeans won't zip, a shoeshine box

I didn't need turned into frustration when I had to move it out of the way as I searched for things I actually did need.

When I couldn't find the thing I needed, I felt frustration and, honestly, self-loathing. Knowing I have something but having no idea which pile it's in is the worst.

Still, I truly believed I valued my stuff. I just *knew* I was somehow more informed and better prepared than other people in the world who didn't have the faintest idea why anyone would ever pay good money (no matter how great a deal she got) for a shoeshine box if she had no intention of ever shining shoes.

I had a gift for seeing value other people couldn't see. Because I loved and valued each individual thing as it came into my home, I assumed I equally valued it as a whole, as stuff.

But even though I believed the items entering my home were valuable, the fact that they lived in a jumbled mess inside my home meant my view of the jumbled mess was skewed. I looked at the pile of random things and felt the overall feeling that everything in it was important. That everything in it had value, so the pile itself was valuable.

Later in this book I'll share exactly how I broke through this feeling and got started, but for now let me just say I was wrong. Every single time and with every single pile.

Once I started going through my piles of valuable stuff, I saw that the ratio was almost always around ten to one. Ten completely obviously (even to me) not-valuable-at-all things to one potentially valuable (to anyone, even me) thing.

As I got rid of obviously worthless stuff, I started realizing I loved something else.

I loved space. Open space. I had no idea how much I would love open space because I'd always filled every space that was mine. Every locker, every apartment, every cabinet was filled with all the stuff I was sure I needed and valued.

As I got rid of things, I was shocked at the shift in my mood when I saw an open space. A shelf with only one or two things on it. The almost empty shelf made me happy because I could really see and enjoy the things left on it. It turned out I liked *that* feeling of actual happiness better than the feeling I got from assuming things on the bottom of a pile were things that would probably make me happy.

> As I got rid of obviously worthless stuff, I started realizing I loved something else.
>
> I loved space.

I loved opening a kitchen cabinet and being able to reach inside and grab exactly what I needed without shifting and looking behind something else or living in fear of it all falling out.

I loved being able to set my table with plates and cups and silverware without having to first spend time clearing the clutter.

I loved being able to sit down at a desk and write, or walk into the laundry room and do laundry.

Life was easier when there weren't piles or boxes everywhere.

I started valuing a lack of stuff.[1]

VALUING SPACE OVER MONEY

My perception of value wasn't only emotional; it was also monetary.

My love of amazing deals on things I might need in the future took a scary (though initially exciting) turn when I started selling online. After I discovered I could *earn* money by bargain shopping, I

---

1. Unfortunately, the shoeshine box example isn't hypothetical. For years I really did have one for the sole purpose of using it in a photo shoot one day. I never used it. I decluttered it.

brought things into my home that I didn't personally want but that I thought someone else might.

And these things (plus everything that was already in my home) now had invisible dollar signs attached to them. Every time I considered getting rid of something, my brain calculated how much money I might get if I sold it.

I already struggled to get things out of my house, and now I analyzed and planned how to milk every last possible penny out of every last possible thing to leave my home.

As I began valuing empty space, room to move without bumping into things, and the ability to glance up without seeing piles of clutter, I finally grew to value space more than the money I could get for my stuff. Changing what I valued also changed the speed at which I could get things out of my home.

In the beginning of this brain transformation, I thought I needed to force myself to forgo possible monetary gain in order to gain open space in my home more quickly. But after I started letting things go, I began to see that empty space has monetary value as well.

I'd always heard organized people casually mention that it's important to think about how much you're willing to pay to store an item.

I had absolutely no idea what they were saying until I started decluttering. As I purged clutter, my house felt bigger.

I had often blamed the size of my house for my clutter problems, so this was bizarre.

One example of this phenomenon is my master bedroom closet. For years it basically was an out-of-control storage unit. When we purchased this home, I was excited to have a walk-in master bedroom closet. Subconsciously, that walk-in master bedroom closet was part of our decision that this house was worth its monthly mortgage payment.

We pay a mortgage for a 2,052-square-foot house. It's not huge, but it's most definitely not small when compared with other houses in the vast majority of the world.

If my closet is 25 square feet, then I'm paying (if I did the math correctly) around ten dollars per month for that space.

I'm willing to pay ten dollars each month to have a nice walk-in closet. I am not willing to pay ten dollars a month to store a bunch of stuff I don't use. And even more important, I am not willing to pay ten dollars each month to store stuff I don't use *and* not be able to walk into the walk-in closet I originally agreed to pay ten dollars a month to have.

Open space makes me like my home more. Boxes and piles of stuff don't.

But I completely understand your skepticism. I didn't believe it either until I experienced it. So, please, experience it.

GETTING REALISTIC ABOUT MY DEBILITATING FRUGALITY

Frugality is a condition I've suffered from since birth. Some days I brag about it; others I suffer its effects. After decluttering huge amounts of amazing bargains from my home, I've had to admit my frugality contributes to my clutter issues.

I must clarify that this particular quirk doesn't necessarily result in someone having a home that's out of control. I know (and greatly admire) people who shop sales for things they'll need in the future and keep their homes beautifully under control. They see the future value something will have for them, buy it at rock-bottom price, put it in a spot they'll remember, and then actually remember it's there when they need it.

Then—and this is the big one—they can *find* it when they need it.

I have shopped with people who do this right, and I've finally admitted what I was doing wrong: I was looking for potential future usefulness while they were spotting definite usefulness that was temporarily put on hold.

They decided something was a bargain if it would solve a problem they'd definitely have in the future. If life went as planned, their three-year-old would one day be five and would need a winter coat for a five-year-old.

I purchased bargains with *potential* usefulness. I bought things as a gamble. I gambled on the chance that one day, my dreams would come true. I would turn into the kind of person who mended expensive but damaged clothing. I would be the tinkerer who repaired a lamp that made guests gasp in delight and hang on my every word as I detailed the restoration process.

My family attended a reunion near a town where we'd lived for four years, so we visited our old church on a Sunday morning. I was delighted to see friends who had endured the baby years with me and catch up on what our teenagers were doing now. As my husband talked with the men, I heard him sheepishly re-apologize for the damage caused to one man's truck when we moved ten years earlier.

I squinted my eyes and tilted my head a little to the right. I had no memory of this incident. The truck's owner didn't remember either, so I listened to my husband explain.

Evidently, these friends (better friends than I even remembered) had helped my husband haul a bathtub to the dump. A cast-iron bathtub. An extremely heavy cast-iron bathtub.

I was completely and totally baffled. *What bathtub?*

According to my husband's story, it was a huge ordeal to load this bathtub (being cast iron and all), and it put a gash into the liner of this man's pickup truck.

The men were laughing about the hilariousness of hauling a bathtub out of the backyard. I was puzzled at my complete lack of any memory whatsoever of this bathtub and embarrassed that something so large and full of hassle could have slipped my mind completely.

I questioned my husband after we left. He didn't remember much other than that we'd hauled a cast-iron bathtub both into and out of our backyard in the years we lived in that house.

Eventually, some vague details came to me. That house was my first experience with premolded, drop-in bathtubs and showers. The plasticky surface felt weird to me and was also harder to clean.

At that time I believed I would one day be as practical and resourceful and DIY handy as the people on the shows I liked to watch. So when my parents remodeled their master bathroom, I was happy to take their perfectly good cast-iron bathtub off their hands and perfectly happy to have someone (I can't remember who) haul it the more-than-two-hours to our house *where it sat for three years until we had to move it because we were moving.*

Through a quick online search, I've learned that cast-iron bathtubs with no fancy features run around $500. I love the idea of saving $500.

Except that we never got around to replacing our bathtub. And we lived with a cast-iron bathtub in our backyard for three years. And we spent our super-helpful friends' energy on loading and hauling to the dump a cast-iron bathtub we'd never needed.

In hindsight, I get how ridiculous it was to keep that bathtub. Having lived eleven years in a different house with the same kind of plasticky bathtubs and never replacing them, I've accepted that I am not a DIYer.

But through decluttering I've also changed my idea of value. Five hundred dollars divided by the three years the bathtub sat in our backyard means we would have saved $166 per year *if we had used it.*

Even if we had used it after three years, was it worth $166 per year to give up the space in our backyard, to have a bathtub as an eyesore, and for my husband to spend time weedeating around it? No.

Was it worth $166 a year in savings to have a bathtub in my backyard?

Again, no.

And was it worth four or five grown men volunteering their time and muscle to haul it to the dump?

Oh my word, no.

I cringe (quite literally) at the thought that I ever truly believed obtaining that bathtub was frugal.

Even though my frugal side still tries to argue with the side of me that understands my reality, I've decided the internal dialogues are well worth my time. An amazing bargain that ultimately makes my life more difficult isn't an amazing bargain at all.

MAKING PROGRESS WITH THE VISIBILITY RULE

Pre-deslobification process, I was overwhelmed by my entire home. Every last space was overflowing with stuff.

I decluttered, but I rarely felt like I made progress, even after putting in hours and hours of work.

Experiencing panic and shortness of breath at the sound of a doorbell is annoying enough on a random day when I'm caught off guard. It's worse than annoying to still feel embarrassed when I've been cleaning or decluttering all day.

If the living room has clutter on every surface and the dining room table is covered with mail, no one automatically thinks, *Wow. Dana has been getting things done today.*

So I created the Visibility Rule: when I declutter, I start with the most visible spaces first. This ensures the results of my efforts will be visible, which will inspire me to keep going, and my decluttering energy will increase instead of being sucked away by a project that gave me nothing to show for my effort.

But whose visibility are we talking about here? What I see every day during my normal, living-in-my-house life? What guests see? What my family sees?

The short answer? Guests. Even if you rarely have guests in your home.

Declutter that most visible area first, every time. The Visibility Rule serves as both a short-term strategy and a long-term strategy. As a short-term strategy, it helps me focus and prioritize. I have a place to start when I'm overwhelmed by the overall mess. *Visibility! Visibility! Visibility!* is a chant I can say in my head to stay on track.

As a long-term strategy, following the Visibility Rule means starting again in the most visible places with each decluttering session. Re-clutterers like me resist this.

How will I ever get to the rest of the house if every decluttering session starts with those same visible spaces? When a space I've decluttered becomes re-cluttered before I get to the next space, or *as I'm working on the next space*, it feels like no progress will ever be made and I'll never get to the spaces where we live our daily lives.

Remember, I'm not sharing simple decluttering hacks in this book. I'm sharing real-life fixes.

In real life, the Visibility Rule plays out like this:

When you're ready to declutter, go to the front door (or whatever door your guests enter). See what your guests see, and start there. Starting in that visible space every time will maintain your overall progress and will (really, I promise) eventually lead to your whole house being decluttered. At the same time.

When I began my own process in 2009, one of my first decluttering projects was my dining room. It's the first thing people see when they walk into my house. Honestly, I was prioritizing according to embarrassment level. I can't share a photo in this book because the camera I used in those early days of blogging was of such low quality the photos would never transfer to print. So let me describe it.

In the photo, I see a red bicycle helmet on top of a pile of papers that almost completely covers the top of my dining room table. The papers include instruction books, newspapers, coupons, and random junk mail. Mixed in with the paper mess, I see a screwdriver, a few socks and other pieces of clothing, a box of checks, a dehydrator, and an onion.

Surely it isn't an onion, but in the photo, it totally looks like an onion.

A chair behind the table appears to be piled high with clothing. A chair in front of the table is definitely covered in clothing. On the floor, there are socks and a large sheet or blanket. There's also a laundry basket and two bicycles.

Yes, I said bicycles.

That was a huge project, but according to the blog post I wrote about it, I spent less than an hour decluttering the room. Looking at that photo, even now as a Seasoned Declutterer, I would have assumed I'd need more than an hour.

But I said something else in that 2009 post that reveals the need to follow the Visibility Rule: "When it's clean, I love this room. It makes me happy to walk by it."

I can successfully not see a mess, even a fairly horrific one, until the doorbell rings. But, strangely, I do see clear spaces. Clear spaces make me happy every time I walk past them, and *that* is the biggest reason I have to follow the Visibility Rule. Following the Visibility Rule means my fleeting decluttering energy won't flee quite so quickly. It will renew itself. Perpetuate.

A room that "makes me happy to walk by it" gives me energy to keep decluttering. When I get a jolt of random decluttering energy and expend it in an invisible space, such as my sock drawer, I use up that energy. It doesn't replenish itself, because I don't see the results of my efforts unless I happen to use that space. That energy is random, not perpetual.

Using my energy on a space I'll see every single day creates visible progress. Visible progress makes energy sustainable.

Which makes decluttering sustainable.

Which, over time, affects my entire home.

But what about the feeling that while I'm focusing on one area of my home, another is getting out of control? How will progress ever happen if I keep going back to work on the same area?

Progress won't happen if I don't.

When I come to my next available time to declutter (which comes sooner since I've been inspired by the loveliness of a decluttered dining room), I still prioritize by visibility, again starting in the entryway and dining room.

When I first decluttered that dining room, it took less than an hour. Significantly less time than I assumed it would take, even though that room was full of decisions to make and habits to break. And the pile was six inches thick and covered the entire table.

That was more than one week's worth of mess. That mess had been building for a very long time.

But when I start again in that visible space after only a week (or a month) as opposed to months (or a year), I'm re-decluttering.

Re-decluttering is shockingly easier than decluttering. I made the hard decisions last time. This time, it's mostly a matter of putting things away. It's mostly easy stuff.

If I have only an hour to give, I can make it back through the dining room in significantly less time than the first decluttering session. What took almost an hour the first time takes ten minutes this time. I have fifty minutes to spend doing hard, first-time-in-a-long-time decluttering on the next visible space.

I now have two spaces that inspire me every time I walk by them. The next time, I start again (yes, really) in my dining room. But this time, it only takes me five minutes (maybe even less).

I've gained experience each time I've worked in there, and with that experience comes a little wisdom. With wisdom, re-cluttering happens less. On a normal, not-decluttering-today day, I recognize junk mail for the future clutter it is and choose to walk straight to the trash can or recycling bin the moment I bring it into my house.

So this third time there are just a few random things to put away.

I move to the second visible space, and after ten minutes of easy re-decluttering in there, I'm ready to go spend forty-five minutes tackling the *next* visible space.

And so on and so forth.

And on and on.

Forever and ever, amen.

The progress is gradual, *but it's visible.* As long as progress is visible, I keep going toward the edges of the house.

Following the Visibility Rule is important, but if you don't, there's no wrong way to declutter. If you're getting stuff out of your house, you're succeeding. If your home functions better, go you! Any decluttering at all is a win for sure.

But if you're constantly frustrated because you can't make sustainable progress, repeat to yourself, *Visibility, visibility, visibility.*

Chapter 6

UNDERSTANDING THE
LAYERS OF A CLEAN HOUSE

If your reaction to cleaning house seems to be vastly different from the reactions of your friends, it's possible that cleaning your house involves peeling back layers that shouldn't be there.

Before I understood these layers, my home was almost always a disaster even though I felt like I was always cleaning. I heard people laugh about how they hated cleaning so much they just never cleaned, but their homes always looked perfectly fine to me.

I now know we were talking about different things. Same words, different (like, completely different) things. There are layers to a clean house, but only one of those layers is actually cleaning.

I was talking about all three layers. They were talking about cleaning.

LAYER ONE: DAILY STUFF

If you read *How to Manage Your Home Without Losing Your Mind*, you know how much of a difference daily stuff made in my quest for a non-disastrous home. Honestly, the daily stuff made *all* the difference. I urge people who are completely overwhelmed to begin with the daily stuff.

When I wasn't doing daily stuff daily, I thought cleaning meant catching up. For me, it did. To clean my house, I had to wash dishes and pick up randomness off the floor and off every flat surface. Sweeping the kitchen floor took at least an hour, because I had to clear it of the junk that collects if I'm not dealing with things like newspapers and empty coffee cans as they appear.

Dealing with daily stuff every day means that when it's time to clean, you get to skip this layer. That makes cleaning so much easier and so much more likely to happen.

LAYER TWO: CLUTTER

The second layer is clutter. As you know from my clutter history, I had a lot of it. I assumed dealing with this stuff was cleaning, because when I cleaned, it was. Dealing with clutter was part of cleaning for me because I couldn't sweep or dust with it there.

Layer two was the layer filled with angst. When I said I hated cleaning, I was talking about this layer. Decluttering requires effort and decision-making and moving past emotional blockades. This meant I put off cleaning as long as I possibly could, and when I was forced to clean because the doorbell was scheduled to ring, I dealt with the clutter level by boxing it up in the garage or shoving everything in the master bedroom and locking the door until whatever event I was cleaning my house for was over.

LAYER THREE: CLEANING

Layer three is cleaning. It's counter-wiping and floor-mopping and surface-dusting and carpet-sweeping. And while it will never be fun, I still find myself shocked by how much easier it is when I don't have to catch up on daily stuff and decluttering (or, honestly, Stuff Shifting) first.

When I had to clean bathrooms but hadn't dealt with layer one (dirty clothes and towels strewn across the floor and random brushes and bottles strewn across the counters) or layer two (clutter with no place to go), this already unfun task was extra frustrating and more time-consuming.

I've had to accept that I can't clean if there's clutter everywhere. I won't go into how to get the daily stuff under control. That's what my other book is for. Just know that daily stuff builds on itself and, left undone, multiplies exponentially.

Cleaning and decluttering are not the same thing. And daily stuff isn't cleaning either. But rather than let yourself get depressed over this fact of life, here's some hope.

This book is all about layer two: decluttering. The beauty of focusing intensely on layer two is that it's the only layer that lasts. Daily stuff has to be done every day for the rest of your life, and the effects of cleaning don't last. Dust falls, toilets get used, and toothpaste splatters on the bathroom mirror. It never ends.

But once something leaves your house, it's gone. And the more things leave, the more that layer becomes a non-issue and makes the other layers so much less overwhelming and quicker to tackle.

The layers of a clean house were amazingly simple once I understood what they were and how I was making my life more difficult by treating them as one big, overwhelming thing instead of as layers.

ONE MORE THING: PROCRASTICLUTTER

Ever feel like you're staying on top of the mess, rocking and rolling with the stuff that is supposed to keep things under control, but your house still looks messy?

The culprit is most likely procrasticlutter.

Procrasticlutter is stuff that's technically (if you're into technicalities, which people with procrasticlutter usually are) not clutter. It's the stuff that will be done one day because it will have to be done one day. It doesn't feel like a daily task, but it also doesn't feel like clutter, so it falls into no-man's-land in the layers of a clean house.

Procrasticlutter, by definition, is made up of things that require no decisions. You already know exactly what to do with procrasticlutter; you just haven't done it.

The most frequent examples of procrasticlutter are clean laundry piled on the couch and clean dishes in the dish drainer or the dishwasher. If the dishes are clean and usable, the task feels finished. If the laundry has been through both the washer and the dryer, it's technically clean. And as someone who adjusts (too) easily to less than perfect situations, grabbing a coffee cup from the top rack of the dishwasher or a pair of socks from the pile on the couch doesn't feel the least bit awkward, so the visible pile doesn't register as a problem.

All this is fine, and life can totally go on this way. Clean dishes and clean laundry are significantly less significant problems than piles of dirty dishes or dirty laundry.

Except that a room with piles, even piles of clean stuff, doesn't look clean. And piles of any kind are like fertilizer for other piles. Piles multiply. The existence of one pile justifies the existence of the next.

But what do you do about them? Well, um, stop procrastinating. The best way to prevent procrasticlutter is to avoid it in the first place. Make putting away clean dishes a part of your daily routine. Fold laundry as you take it out of the dryer or off the line, and put it away immediately.

But when you don't (because if you're anything like me, there will be times you don't), don't skip over procrasticlutter in the decluttering process (layer two). Dealing with procrasticlutter will come up again and again in every room we work through in this book.

Procrasticlutter needs its own explanation because even in the midst of decluttering mode, putting off dealing with it (procrastinating) makes so much sense. Shouldn't I use my decluttering energy on real decluttering instead of on these tedious daily things?

Yes, except this daily stuff is clutter because you haven't been dealing with it daily. If you dive into the tough decluttering stuff and ignore the procrasticlutter, you'll feel like your efforts were wasted even though you worked all day. The room will still look messy.

But if you do the easy stuff first and deal with the procrasticlutter, at the end of the day you'll see progress. The room will look better. Seeing progress is so much better than telling yourself you made progress even though you can't see it.

Chapter 7

GETTING IT OUT, OR THE CASE FOR THE DONATE BOX

I'm a big fan of donating. I totally understand if you're not because it took me a *long* time to come to that point, but know that all decluttering advice in this book will include instructions to "stick it in the Donate Box."

I have done it all. I have milked every dollar out of my stuff by selling it on eBay. I've sold on Craigslist and through Facebook groups. I've been a member of Freecycle (a group where you are only allowed to give things away for free), and I've held multiple garage sales in one year.

While I did all of those, I struggled with clutter. I lived way above my Clutter Threshold, and clutter was a constant source of stress in my home.

As I shifted into the mode of fast and furious decluttering, I began selling less and donating more. And once I stopped worrying about how much money I could get for things, I started making major progress.

SPEEDY DECLUTTERING

The biggest advantage of donating is the speed at which I get stuff out of my house.

When I donate, I'm (almost) done the moment I place an item in a Donate Box. There is no work left to do other than take a trip to a local charity or make a phone call to schedule a pickup.

There's physical work involved in getting stuff out of my house, but there is no scheming or analyzing or calculating to be done. Scheming and analyzing and calculating get me into trouble.

When I shifted into almost exclusively donating, the stuff was gone from my house soon after I decided it needed to go. Selling on eBay required a holding area where things could stay until I had the time (and the season was right) to sell them. But a space like that was beyond the limitations of my Clutter Threshold. I love looking at rows and shelves of perfectly organized and labeled containers, but I can't keep that up in my own home.

Having a garage sale meant a garage piled high with junk while I collected enough stuff to make the effort worth my while and found a Saturday with no soccer games or swim meets.

Even idealistic giving away was a problem for me. Giving things to the perfect person who would perfectly appreciate my thoughtfully unloaded clutter involved a detailed, complicated system of sorting.

As I went through bins and bins of my kids' clothing, I wasn't only deciding which things to keep. I also had to determine which way I was going to get rid of them.

My idealistic logic said clothes that have been given to us as hand-me-downs by nonfamily members should be given away. I didn't feel right selling them, so I made piles for random people I knew who had kids in whatever ages the clothes might fit.

Hand-me-downs from family and gifted clothing could be sold. But even that wasn't a single pile. I analyzed each item for trendiness and flaws. If it was in perfect condition, I could sell it on eBay. If it had flaws, I'd put it in my garage sale.

Every time I decluttered kids' clothing, I ended up with an entire bed covered in piles. And no one could help me because I was the only one who understood my nuanced system.

Once the piles were made, it wasn't over. The eBay piles and the garage-sale piles needed separate holding areas to wait until their ideal selling times arrived. Piles going to various people had to be bagged separately, the people had to be contacted, and I had to remember to take them their things.

And remember how remembering really isn't my thing?

My system for everything else (other than clothing) was equally complicated. (Who could use this? How much money could I get for this? What's the best way to sell this?) But nonclothes couldn't be bagged up and thrown in a corner. They had to be wrapped or placed somewhere where they wouldn't be damaged while they waited to leave my home.

Worst of all, my effort often made my home look worse. Piles and stacks sat in the open, waiting for their Ideal Decluttering Method to happen.

When I began decluttering like my sanity depended on it, I simply did not have time to use my complicated systems. I just donated.

When I donated, I didn't have to remember where this particular onesie came from. I could stick it in the Donate Box. I didn't have to examine every seam and hold each romper up to the light to check for slight discoloration. Anything could be donated. No moral judgments needed. Donating is always acceptable.[1]

---

1. If you are upset by this statement, don't worry. I'll share more about what's okay to donate and what's not in the Decluttering Room By Room chapters.

Once I made the decision to donate everything, I felt incredible freedom, and I was able to move through my clutter so much more quickly. I made the decision about whether something needed to stay in my house or not, and that was the end of it.

FINDING A PLACE TO DONATE

When I stopped sorting and started donating, my progress accelerated. But where should you donate? My main criteria for a donation place is that they take everything and don't require me to sort.

But how do you *find* a place to donate? Ask.

You can search on the Internet, but many charities do not have a detailed online presence that explains their particular policies, and there's nothing worse than trying to donate a carload of stuff and being turned away.

Ask friends who live in your town. Don't be embarrassed. *People whose homes aren't cluttered know how to get rid of their stuff.* They know where to take donations. It's probably so normal to them that they won't think twice about you asking. You don't have to give details or explain that you've been living above your Clutter Threshold. Use social media: "Hey, local friends, where do you donate things?"

> Once I made the decision to donate everything, I felt incredible freedom, and I was able to move through my clutter so much more quickly.

I live in a small town without a ton of options, and I still learn new ways to get rid of things when I ask or see other people ask.

But when? Establishing the routine of stopping by a local charity every Wednesday at three o'clock to get rid of that week's donations is a great idea. Really. That idea is totally on my Someday When I Have It All Together List. But if you're anything like me, you know that would likely mean driving around with the first week's donations sitting in the trunk of your car for a year and a half.

For now, while you're in Major Decluttering Mode, load your *entire* vehicle with donations or call a local donation pickup service to schedule a pickup.

CONSIDER THE HASSLE FACTOR

Because of the Internet, there are a million ways to get rid of things, for free or for sale. Freecycle.org is a group that was around before Facebook groups were a thing. I found a local group early in my post-eBay-selling and pre-donate-it-all days. I thought that group was the answer to my problems. I would give things away. And doing it through this Freecycle group would ensure that my amazingly awesome things wouldn't go to waste. They would go to someone who really needed them, and I would have some control over that.

But there was hassle involved.

Even though I was giving things away, I was giving them away one item at a time. Each item required a description and photo to be posted online. That post had to be monitored for responses. I had to coordinate pickups, and this often meant multiple e-mails back and forth with a second or third person after the first or second person decided they didn't want it.

If I posted something lots of people wanted, I had to figure out who claimed it first. Sometimes I had to defend that decision to the people who weren't first.

All that hassle meant I *intended* to use this amazing Internet-age resource to get rid of my stuff, but I put off actually using it.

And then there was the issue of my own excitement over free stuff. I was a recovering junk addict. For years I brought things into my home without considering the harm it was doing to my home, my family, and our well-being. Now I was trying to get stuff out, but being in a Freecycle group was, to me, like an alcoholic hanging out in a bar.

I've had the same experience in the more currently relevant Facebook swap/buy-and-sell/everything-is-free groups. The best way for me to get stuff out of my house quickly, and without emotional hassle, is to donate.

It just is.

Chapter 8

CHANGING YOUR MIND-SET CHANGES YOUR HOME

I had already started decluttering when I first heard the term *minimalism*. I pictured empty rooms and one-pot kitchens and closets with one shirt, one pair of pants, and maybe a jacket.

Honestly, I pictured a college apartment. Specifically, the one where some of my guy friends lived.

In that basement apartment we sat around for hours on end, watching movies on a television that was balanced on a TV tray. There was one old couch and, at the most, one spaghetti pot. Not that we ever cooked there.

As people on the Internet started calling themselves minimalists, though, I saw they were talking about a much sleeker and stylish lifestyle than I'd pictured inside my head.

Minimalism is a trendy topic these days. I, as a rule, am not trendy.

But as I decluttered, the term came to my mind often. I liked the idea and realized that with my Clutter Threshold, I needed to aim for minimalism. I function better with less stuff in my home.

But here's the problem. As the world in general rebels against excess, millennials with no kids and location-independent jobs have embraced the beauty of living with the bare minimum. For people who start adulthood this way, or for people who have naturally been living well within their Clutter Thresholds, this will result in a home with just enough, a home that is comfortable and easy to maintain.

But what about those of us who can't fit our large families (large in number and large in size) into a tiny house we tote around the country at will? And, honestly, what about those of us who are just now seeing the beauty of a minimalist lifestyle and longing to live without the encumbrance of stuff but can't even imagine how we'll go about getting rid of everything we maniacally collected before we learned that minimalism was a thing, much less an attractive thing?

I've shared that my husband and I started our marriage with an apartment already bulging at the seams with stuff. We have two close friends, though, whose journey with stuff as a couple looked very different.

Like me, she had lived overseas for a few years before they married. Like my husband, he had also lived on his own. But when they got married, their apartment held one set of treasured dishes, a couch, a washer and dryer, and a bed. There must have been a pot or a pan, but that was about it.

A few people sat on the couch, and the rest of us sat on the floor. We watched a TV propped up on a box or some other completely unfancy contraption. We ate in those same positions, and every one of my memories of their newlywed apartment is perfectly happy and fun.

I remember clearly when they added things to their apartment. I remember a curtain, a large decorative mirror, and a table. I remember because each addition of a new item was a big deal.

I also remember when they bought another table to replace their first one.

The first table they had as a married couple was thanks to me. Another friend mentioned she was giving away her old table, so I connected these two friends and thought very highly of myself for solving everyone's problems.

But then a few months later I arrived at my friends' bare-bones apartment and found a *different* table. This table was new. They'd searched and searched until they found exactly the table they wanted. As the self-proclaimed table-finding hero, I asked where they'd put the old (but still new to them) one.

They'd given it away.

I was puzzled, and they were puzzled that I was puzzled.

I couldn't understand. How could you give away something you just got? Something so perfectly useful? They couldn't understand why anyone *wouldn't* give away something, even if they just got it, if they bought something that logically replaced it.

This way of thinking was completely foreign to my brain.

Almost twenty years into the future, they have added a carefully chosen, just-right piece almost every time we visit, and their home is exactly how they want it. Except for the table I forced on them, they have made a conscious decision to avoid temporary solutions to problems that could technically be solved by going without.

Because getting rid of things is a hassle. Getting rid of big things is a big hassle. They chose to live without something until they truly knew they needed it and knew exactly how it would function in their home because they'd lived in that home.

We, on the other hand, have purged multiple homes' worth of stuff and still have more to go. And we know all about the hassle of getting rid of things. Even really cool things.

Like the foosball table I bought at a garage sale because foosball tables are cool. I'd never thought about needing a foosball table until the moment I saw it at that sale. And since I'd never thought about having one, I'd never thought about where we'd put one.

That table was an albatross around my neck for years. The kids played with it occasionally when it was out in the middle of the room and they could get to the rods on each side. The long and pokey rods that slid back and forth whenever we tried to move it. We rarely kept the table out in the middle of the room where people could actually play, because the rods were extremely painful to run into—and we ran into them often. There simply wasn't enough space for the table and open space around it so we could use the room for all the other purposes we'd used it for before bringing home the surprise foosball table. Finally, we moved the table to our back patio, and eventually we took it to the dump. I felt bad for dumping it, but it turns out that other people aren't as eager to take home a for-occasional-fun-only, furniture-sized item, and I couldn't find anyone who wanted it.

I could use up all sixty thousand words of this book listing other things that were a hassle to remove from our home.

Bringing useful things into the house is fun, and using them is satisfying. Bringing random things into the house is also fun, but when there's no use for them they're not fun. They're in the way, and they make living in the house unfun. Having to get rid of things, especially bulky, heavy things, is the complete opposite of fun.

Through my friends' example I understand how minimalism works in real life, but how do you embrace this concept when you're so far away from a minimal home?

It's a mind-set. And the mind-set is that life is better and easier with less. And it's better to live without something you might use than to have something you don't use. Start erring on the side of getting rid of things. Be willing to risk not having something that you truly might wish you had one day.

Maybes are nos.

What-ifs become let's-assume-probably-nots.

And wouldn't-it-be-nice-to-haves turn into I'm-sure-I-could-get-replacements.

Mind-set. That's what this is. A change in my perspective. A difference in my ultimate goal for my home. A desire to have less stress by having less stuff.

But decluttering with this mind-set is actually about *keeping* stuff. Huh?

The definition of *decluttering* is getting rid of things I don't need. But the point of decluttering is to keep stuff.

The goal is a home free of clutter, right? A home where everyday living is easy and enjoyable, and my family can do the things we need to do without tripping over random junk.

So many times, I fought the irrational desire for my home to burn down to the ground along with every nonliving thing in it (while all people and animals were perfectly safe, of course). I know that's pretty much the definition of crazy, but it's also the definition of desperation.

Being completely overwhelmed made me feel the only option was for it *all* to go.

My house full of stuff was a huge project. A bajillion different little decisions that I needed to make. Getting started was hard because of the sheer volume of work that would be required. So starting from nothing seemed like the best idea.

Except that starting from nothing wasn't an option, which made starting that much harder to consider.

I have a family. We need things. We definitely don't need as many things as we had, but we do need things: pots to boil water in, clothes to wear, chairs to sit in, and even a few things to entertain us. And honestly, there are things I love. Things I cherish.

When I declutter, I feel happy as things leave my home. The literal weight of that stuff is gone, and I'm thrilled to have open space.

But I also find joy in the things I keep.

I keep the things we need and love, guilt free, because I've accepted the size of the container that is my house and acknowledged that these treasured things deserve space in that container more than other things that I didn't love.

And something beautiful happens: the things I love have room to breathe, and this lets me breathe as well. The things I love are now visible, and the things I need are now findable, not crowded out by a mass of stuff I don't even care about.

So the point of decluttering isn't to get rid of things you want to keep; it's to identify those things and then to make space to enjoy those things.

USEFULNESS AND USING STUFF

There's a difference between something being useful and actually using something. It's kind of a big difference. One of my favorite and most effective decluttering strategies has been to justify keeping things by using them.

Between 2003 and 2006 something happened in the world of baby products: monograms and colorful fabrics turned things like burp cloths into designer keepsakes. With kid #1, people just gave advice like, "Hey, know what's a good idea? Have a burp cloth!"

So as we moved out of the baby stage, I was weighed down with the decision about what to do with precious cloth diapers monogrammed with my daughter's name. Could I, in my desperate determination to purge the clutter from my overfilled home, *keep* burp cloths when my kids were past the stage of burping onto such things?

I kept them, but I also used them. Using them freed me to keep these keepsakes without guilt. I used monogrammed burp cloths for cleaning bathrooms or wiping down toys. I sopped up spills with them, and every time I did, I enjoyed their unique color combos and memories of baby snuggles.

And now? Honestly, I have no idea where they are. Because here's the thing I've realized as I have decided to use things instead of store them: once I use things, I use them up, and then the pain of decluttering isn't so harsh. This goes back to the concept of Decluttering Paralysis, and how the best cure for it is to move.

I lay small blankets that were pushing out of the edges of a trunk (breaking out of their container) across the backs of seats and couches so my family could use them on winter evenings when Mama wasn't quite ready to turn up the heat.

I drank from random commemorative mugs and glasses and plastic souvenir cups.

My perspective began to change. I learned which things produced great memories with every single sip or snuggle. But I also learned that a cup with a funny ridge loses its coolness and sentimental appeal when I feel irritated every time I use it. I couldn't part with that cup when I pulled it out of a box full of memories, but it is the first to go when I declutter the cabinet where it sits ignored in favor of better cups.

And somehow, even if an item turns out to be extremely useful, I'm so much more willing to get rid of it once it's used up. Once the design has been rubbed away or the fabric is threadbare, I feel a sense of completion, of a job well done.

USE IT OR LOSE IT

But what about *potential* usefulness? About stuff that could be useful *if* . . .

If I fixed it. If I ordered the missing part off the Internet. If I cleaned it up or painted it a color I like, or even if I just pulled it out of the big pile of other random, potentially useful stuff sitting in the garage.

I was the queen of loving things and valuing things for their potential usefulness. I focused on what things could be, and I ignored the reality of what they were (or weren't) in my home.

I decided to keep the things I use and let go of useful things I didn't actually use.

I can come up with reasons why something is useful. I can brainstorm fifteen uses for an old table leg in fifteen minutes or less.

But when I'm not asking myself if something is useful, but telling myself to start using it, then I have a choice: I can order a lamp kit and start stringing wire through the table leg the minute the kit arrives, or I can declutter that old, tableless table leg.

Decluttering is way easier than building table-leg lamps.

DECLUTTERING AT
THE SPEED OF LIFE

I'm about to head into the section of the book with step-by-step decluttering instructions. Don't get overwhelmed and stop reading. These instructions work whether you're planning to declutter twelve hours a day for seven days straight, or you only have five minutes today and seven minutes tomorrow and who knows what will happen after that.

And that's the beauty of decluttering at the speed of life—your real life.

I suffer from TPAD (Time Passage Awareness Disorder). It is a disorder I made up, but it's totally real. It means I rarely have a realistic understanding of how much time a certain activity will take. I assume it will take more time than I have, or I assume it will go faster than it ends up going.

I almost never assume correctly, and this used to make my attempts at decluttering unsuccessful and frustrating.

I have had to create strategies that don't depend on me being able to predict how much time I have to give. Because if there's one thing that is certain about life, it's that it rarely goes as predicted.

I used to wait for each day off, each vacation, each not-a-normal-day to declutter. When those came and went without me making significant progress, I assumed I would finally declutter in the next phase of my life. When I wasn't working full-time. When my kids were older and wouldn't undo any progress I made.

Focused days (sometimes weeks) did occasionally happen, but my efforts didn't make the visible impact I hoped they'd make, and I often ended up with an unfinished decluttering project that made it harder to live in that space. And because I was rarely successful when I had *large* pockets of time to focus, I saw no point in even trying to declutter if I only had a short amount of time.

HOW TO DECLUTTER IN WHATEVER CHUNK OF TIME YOU HAVE

My decluttering strategies are designed to work in the face of distractions. I am a more-than-typically-distractible person, so I created strategies that keep me from ever getting into a situation where, when something distracts me from the decluttering project, I'm worse off than I was before I started. These same strategies allow me to make measurable progress in only five minutes. (Or less.)

As I touch each item, I make a final decision about that item. There are no halfway points, no put-it-here-for-nows, no Procrastination Stations.

Here's how it works. The only supplies you need to start decluttering are a black trash bag (black, so people living in your house won't be able to see what's inside and suddenly remember why they totally need it), a donatable Donate Box (the box itself has to leave the house along with the stuff inside), and your feet (in most cases, attached to the ends of your legs).

Each and every item will go in the trash, in the Donate Box, or in its home. If it doesn't have an established home (like most of my stuff didn't), my two simple decluttering questions will either give it one or help you see it needs to go.

Decluttering Question #1: If I needed this item, where would I look for it first? Take it there right now. The key word is *would*, which is a question of instinct. No pondering or thinking or analyzing needed. The second part of question #1 is ridiculously important. Take it, right now, to the place where you'd look first.

Decluttering Question #2: If I needed this item, would it ever occur to me that I already had one? This needn't be asked if question #1 has an answer. *If there is no answer to question #1*, it's likely because I wouldn't look for it because I didn't even know I had it. If the answer to this question is no, I stick it in the Donate Box.

And that is how you declutter without making a bigger mess. No matter when you stop, you've made progress. In a perfect world, with a guaranteed three days available to devote to decluttering, what makes sense is to pull everything out of a space and then only put back what has a home. But no one I know lives in a perfect world. As long as the take-it-there-now principle is followed, the mess gets smaller and doesn't become a bigger mess outside the space that once held the clutter. This also allows measurable progress to be achieved, even if you get interrupted.

> To declutter at the speed of life, you have to accept that life happens.

To declutter at the speed of life, you have to accept that life happens. By making a final decision about the fate of each item as you pick it up and then acting on that decision (trashing it, donating it, or taking it where it goes immediately), at any point when you get distracted, you've made progress. There are no Keep Piles or Keep Boxes to deal with later.

This means if you have a full day to declutter, you will make a *lot* of progress. You'll do a lot of walking around your house, but at the end of the day, when you feel like you can't look at another Santa figurine, you don't have to. You're done. Whenever you feel like stopping or you have to stop because one of your kids needs you, you can stop with nothing hanging over your head to do later.

So work through all the decluttering steps for your kitchen if you have an entire day to devote to your kitchen. Or work on step 1 if you only have five minutes.

Those five minutes will be totally worth your time.

FIVE MINUTES

I used "five minutes" as an example of a short amount of time because five-minute awkward pauses happen most days. Telling yourself it's worth the effort to declutter for only five minutes is also a great way to get started.

I know how overwhelming a house full to the brim with clutter feels. I know how trying to match up the volume of mess with enough space on the calendar to tackle that volume of mess makes you feel like there's no hope for your home.

When you feel that way, set your timer for five minutes, and start with the first step to dealing with an overwhelming mess: trash. Throw away trash for five minutes, and you will be shocked at how much of an impact you can make on your home in a short amount of time.

If you don't believe me, please try to prove me wrong. Take a photo, set a timer for five minutes, and start working; then take another photo when the timer goes off. Either you'll be happy because you proved me wrong, or you'll be ecstatic because you made a visible impact on your home in only five short minutes. Either way, you win.

LESS IS GOOD AND BETTER IS GOOD

Decluttering perfectly is an unattainable dream for people like me, and knowing just how unattainable it is can be paralyzing. Following the decluttering strategies, in order, for whatever amount of time you have available will result in less stuff in your home. *Less* is good. Accepting the value of less allowed me to start, knowing I'd succeed even if *less* was all I had to show for my effort.

Like *less*, the word *better* was a game changer for me. Ideas flow from my brain like water from a firehose that has lost its regulating valve thingy. My big ideas are sometimes so far from my reality, though, that I'm stuck doing nothing for a long time. When I gave up on waiting until I had time to make things perfect, I was shocked at the value of *better*.

My own big ideas can be the biggest contributors to my Decluttering Paralysis. Envisioning perfection inhibits more than it inspires.

Give yourself permission to just declutter. Don't worry about getting organized, and focus on getting the things you don't need out of your home.

PART 2

Decluttering Room by Room

Chapter 10

STEPS FOR WORKING THROUGH AN OVERWHELMING MESS

You're overwhelmed. I get it. I totally get it. I still sometimes find myself staring into a space and wishing with every wishbone in my body that I could just pretend the mess didn't exist. That I could turn around, close the closet or cabinet or bedroom door, and convince myself that space didn't exist.

But I can't.

In the beginning, every single space in my home was overwhelming to me. I was living so far above my Clutter Threshold that every

> I still sometimes find myself staring into a space and wishing with every wishbone in my body that I could just pretend the mess didn't exist.

drawer and every room felt like a reason for a nervous breakdown. Now those paralyzing spaces are far fewer, and my decluttering confidence has grown significantly. But I still go back to these steps when I work through a cluttered space.

These steps work.

STEP 1: TRASH
(THE EASIEST OF THE EASY STUFF)

Trash is easy. Starting with the most visible mess, I remove trash. There is no running around like there will be in step 2, so it goes extremely quickly. If the mess is three feet deep, I just get the trash that I can see without moving anything else.

Examples of trash: brochures, broken stuff, and actual trash that missed the trash can sitting nearby and then blended with the overwhelming mess.

STEP 2: DO THE EASY STUFF

Easy stuff is the stuff that has an established home somewhere else but for whatever reason isn't there. When I look at a mass of random clutter, it's all overwhelming. But if I ask myself what's easy, I can usually identify one to seven things that don't require any decision because I know where they're supposed to be.

This step includes any procrasticlutter. *Sorry.*

Once I remove the easy stuff, the volume of the mess is reduced, and the space is slightly less overwhelming.

STEP 3: *DUH* CLUTTER

Stick *Duh* Clutter (or *Duh*s) in the Donate Box. *Duh* Clutter shouldn't be a thing, but it totally is. It's the stuff that at the first quick glance I know is clutter. Not much explanation needed here, other than that it's the stuff that makes me go, *Duh. Why do I have that?*

Examples of *Duh* Clutter: Things I thought I already decluttered. Things I have always hated.

STEP 4: ASK THE TWO
DECLUTTERING QUESTIONS

Decluttering Question #1: If I needed this item, where would I look for it first? Take it there now.

Decluttering Question #2: If I needed this item, would it ever occur to me that I already had one?

Take things to the place where you'd look for them first, immediately, if you can answer question #1. (If you can answer the first question, you don't even have to ask the second question.) If you have to ask question #2 and the answer is no, stick the item in the Donate Box.

If you're taking something to where you'd look for it first, glance (but don't dig) at the overall mess to see if there is anything else that obviously goes to that same place. Example: ponytail holders. If there's one, there are probably sixty-five.

Step 4 is where you'll spend the most time while decluttering, asking yourself one or both of the decluttering questions about each item in that space. Be aware, though, that you'll likely uncover more easy stuff, *Duh*s, and trash as you continue working. That's normal. Trash goes in the black trash bag, *Duh*s go straight into the Donate Box, and easy stuff goes where it goes, skipping the two decluttering questions because you don't need them.

STEP 5: MAKE IT FIT

This is the step where you apply the Container Concept to the space where you're working.

Some decluttering projects may not include this step, if the project was only a space-clearing one. Examples of a space-clearing project include cleaning out the random stuff that collects under a couch or clearing a pile of papers from the kitchen counter.

Use step 5 in any decluttering project that involves a container, and remember that a container is anything that holds stuff. Shelves, drawers, and such are containers.

At this point in the process, you've removed all the things that obviously don't belong in this space. Now it's time to purge stuff that *does* belong in this space.

Or *would* belong in this space if you lived in a fantasy world where bookshelves grew as you came home with more books. But you don't live in a fantasy world with magically expanding bookcases. I'm so sorry. I wish I lived there too.

If removing the stuff that obviously didn't belong here left you with a perfectly neat and not-even-a-little-bit-overstuffed space, awesome. You can move on to the next mess.

But if the space is still cluttered, you'll have to keep purging. Step 5.1 will help you do that without shedding a (or many) tear(s).

Step 5.1: Consolidate

This sub-step is slightly more difficult because of my refusal to pull everything out. But once I declutter the obvious trash, easy stuff, and *Duh* Clutter, there's usually enough room to move things around within the space.

I start putting like things together, consolidating. As I do this—as I touch and look at individual things—my eyes will often be opened to trash and easy stuff and *Duh* Clutter I didn't notice in the previous steps. That's perfectly fine. I deal with them in the same way I dealt with them earlier.

Step 5.2: Purge Down to the Limits of the Container

Consolidating opens my eyes to how much of something I have. If you're anything like me, you can feel like you are almost out of sandwich bags until consolidating reveals there are actually four boxes in the cabinet—and three of those boxes are less than half full. So if you combine the bags into one or two boxes, you'll be decluttering two of those boxes, and you'll have less in that cabinet.

But consolidating isn't enough. While sandwich bags are totally useful and will most likely be used eventually, the size of the cabinet where you keep them is the size of the cabinet where you keep them. And it can only hold so many boxes of sandwich bags.

And that cabinet might also need to hold plastic wrap and wax paper and aluminum foil and freezer bags and lunch sacks. And if it does, all those things have to fit in the container that is that cabinet. It's not a question of how many boxes of aluminum foil you should have; it's a question of how many boxes of aluminum foil *will fit on your shelf.*

Purge the ones that don't fit.

If that's hard, look at it this way: Fill the shelf first with the most container-worthy items. If you have a huge number of boxes of storage bags, there's a chance some aren't the brand you like. They were the box you grabbed because you desperately needed some, but it was the day before payday and your grocery budget was spent. Then you grabbed another box of the good ones the next time you went to the store but never got rid of the old ones.

The good ones are container worthy, and the ones you don't like go in the Donate Box. They simply don't fit.

USING THE STEPS TO WORK THROUGH AN ENTIRE (MESSY) ROOM

In this section of the book, I will talk you through these steps in each of the following rooms: living areas, kitchen, bedrooms, closets, craft/hobby rooms (or spaces), and storage spaces.

Warning: I am going to repeat these exact steps for each of those spaces. Every step, every time. I'll get into specific examples and challenges that are unique to each space, but by the time this book is over, you'll have the steps memorized.

And that's pretty much the point. Every home is different, and every space has its own challenges. But the same steps work no matter the clutter and no matter the depth of that clutter. There's no need to reinvent the process every time you start. Just follow the steps.

Your home's layout is unique, but I've ordered the following chapters to follow the Visibility Rule.

> **The same steps work no matter the clutter and no matter the depth of that clutter.**

You might ask, when do you open up cabinets and drawers within those rooms and purge those spaces?

That's up to you.

My advice is to go through the steps, focusing first on all *visible* clutter in the room, working on floors and surfaces and open shelves. Purge visible trash, easy stuff, and *Duhs* from the room as a whole, and then work through individual piles or corners of stuff that are out in the open.

Once you've decluttered all the visible clutter in that room, it's up to you whether you move on to tackle visible surfaces in the next room or stay in that first (most visible) room to clear out its hidden spaces.

Either way is fine. Personally, I like to do out-in-the-open clutter first, room by room, and then begin working on hidden spaces, starting with those visible rooms first.

But what about cleaning?

You read the chapter where I explained that cleaning and decluttering are not the same thing, right? And you know the focus of this book is decluttering and decluttering alone. But I know how hard it can be to reveal a nest of dust bunnies and *not* stop to pull out the cleaning supplies.

One of the biggest perks of decluttering is that you'll be able to clean more easily and much more quickly when you don't have to get clutter out of the way first. But if you must deal with the dust bunnies now, keep it simple. Add a duster (or a clean, unmatched sock) and a vacuum or broom to your decluttering supplies. Quickly run these things over super dusty places as you uncover them, and the space will look so much better. Wait to deep clean until after you've decluttered, lest you get distracted.

Chapter 11

LIVING AREAS

Now that we're going room by room, I'm starting with living areas. Any guesses why?

They're visible. In my home, living areas are the rooms where we sit, watch TV, play games, and entertain guests. We *live* in them.

Honestly, they're the rooms I clean when adults are coming to visit, the spaces without shuttable (or, even better, lockable) doors that I truly can't avoid letting people see.

DEFINE THE ROOM

Living areas, pre-deslobification process, were rooms of randomness. You can start decluttering before you define a room, but knowing a room's purpose helps. We have three rooms I call living areas: our living room, our game room, and our dining room.

The purposes of the living room and dining room were pretty obvious, but the game room was a pain to figure out. That room was a constant mess and a constant frustration, mostly because I referred to it consistently as our office/game room/guest room. (Yes, I spoke the slashes out loud.)

The room had multiple, not-really-congruent purposes. There was a bed in the corner for guests. I put it up against the wall with pillows at the back, hoping that made it look couch-ish. But no one ever used it as a couch. Since the room was also supposed to be an office, a tall desk unit with built-in shelving sat against one wall. Both the bed and the desk were always covered in random stuff.

As I shared this room's progress, setbacks, and frustrations on my blog, helpful readers encouraged me to pick a purpose. To admit this room's ambiguous definition was really an excuse to make it a dumping ground.

They were right. I started calling the space our game room. Even though our desktop computer stayed in there and guests slept on a sofa sleeper, defining that room as a game room took me further in that room's battle against clutter than anything else ever had.

Two things happen when a room isn't defined: it becomes a storage room (and stoqrage rooms aren't good places to hang out or to sleep), or it becomes a dumping ground for temporary things that become less temporary and eventually turn into storage.

Our living room is the place where we hang out as a family. Anything that stays in there needs to contribute to achieving that family-time goal. The dining room has to function as a space to dine. Our dining table is the main item in the room, and it can't get crowded out by things that make dining in there more difficult.

Defining a room colors my decluttering decisions and gives me an end goal.

But if you don't know the room's purpose, don't worry. Declutter anyway. The answer might reveal itself to you as you go.

STEP 1: TRASH

In an ideal world, there wouldn't be trash in the living room. I don't live in an ideal world. Trash in my living room includes things like a stack of school papers left on the coffee table after signing the Tuesday Folder, packaging materials from a new remote control for the TV, and the broken lamp we replaced but somehow never actually got out of the house. And a whole lot of other random stuff.

STEP 2: EASY STUFF

Our living room is a halfway point for things that enter the house but don't get put to use right away. A box of cereal someone dropped on the couch as they brought in groceries. (I have no idea why, either.) Clean laundry piled high or the partially assembled vacuum cleaner along with the box it came in. (Procrasticlutter.)

Take a thing where it goes as soon as you come across it. Some people call this part *picking up*. Or *tidying*. Or *seriously-how-does-any-adult-not-do-this-everyday stuff*. Whatever it's called, do it.

If you're balking at the idea of making a separate trip to take each thing to its already established home, try this: as you pick up something and know where you need to take it, glance around to see if anything else that's *obvious* goes to that place too. If so, grab the obvious thing and take it with you.

Keep doing what you're doing. The Easy Stuff step is removing the top layer of the mess.

STEP 3: *DUH* CLUTTER

Identify *Duh* donations. Look around for stuff you never liked but for some reason were waiting to get rid of until you were in a decluttering mood. Well, you're in the mood now.

While we're talking about decluttering *Duh*s, let's talk about furniture. Big stuff. Entire tables or cabinets or chairs. Or even couches.

Furniture is expensive, and it's supposed to be useful. I move it to a new spot, hoping that putting the table there will make my life better—the way I envisioned it would when I bought it. But when it doesn't, I move the table again.

And then again.

Is that very large item causing more problems than it's solving? Getting rid of big stuff is a big pain, but there's also a big benefit. The room immediately feels bigger and less cramped. And the big thing's nonexistence will mean there's no surface to pile stuff on.

STEP 4: ASK THE DECLUTTERING QUESTIONS

Head to the most visible place in the room with clutter to be purged. At this point, you're decluttering pile by pile.

At the first pile, start with another easy check: Is anything easy lurking on top of this pile that didn't register in your brain when you were looking at the room as a whole? At any phase of any decluttering project, *always* be on the lookout for easy stuff.

If something isn't easy, ask the decluttering questions.

Decluttering Question #1: If I Needed This Item, Where Would I Look for It First?

Trust your instinct. Where *would* you look for it? The first place that pops in your head is the answer to the question, so that's where you take it right now.

But let's go ahead and deal with some snarky resistance to this question. What if you'd look for pliers in the living room? If you'd look in a particular drawer, put them there. But if you'd just look "in the living room" on the hearth or the coffee table, no.

I get it. The house has been bonkers for so long. Even though you'd never put pliers on the coffee table on purpose because they're *pliers*, and it's the *coffee table*, you'd look there first because the living room is the first place you look for everything.

But really, you're being snarky, right? And you bought a book about decluttering. You paid money because you were desperate enough for help that you decided to *read* about *decluttering*. That's not exactly escapism.

Get over the snark and ask yourself where you'd look for this item other than where you found it. Because here, it's clutter. It's in a pile. Where would you look first if this room wasn't a crazy mess?

Let me clarify one more thing to be sure you're asking the entire question correctly. Where would you *look* for it? Not where would you *stick* it. "Where would I stick this?" was the question I asked myself again and again before the deslobification process. *That question doesn't work.*

That question is the reason I had a kitchen junk drawer full of thirty-plus ponytail holders.

We never (and I do mean *never*) look for ponytail holders in the kitchen junk drawer. Those thirty-plus ponytail holders sat in the junk drawer while we desperately searched the house for one. We walked past the kitchen junk drawer again and again without ever considering looking in there for a ponytail holder.

My goal is to be able to find what I need in the moment I need it, without trying to remember what I might have been thinking in the midst of a crazy and frantic cleaning session.

Be Prepared for Distractions

In real life, distractions happen. Resist the urge to be super-duper efficient and throw everything into a box so you can deliver items to their "where would I look first?" homes on one big trip through the house at the end of the project.

Keep Boxes don't work. They let me put off making a final decision. I can temporarily place a particularly difficult item inside, confident that the future version of me will know what to do with it. Future Me doesn't deserve that much credit, and honestly, she doesn't appreciate the pressure.

Keep Boxes let me justify waiting to put things away. They're neat little procrastination holders. I'm still working through Keep Boxes that have been in my garage since we moved twelve years ago. If I put things away immediately, I'm done. If I stick things in a Keep Box, I have "empty that Keep Box" on my mental to-do list indefinitely.

Keep Piles don't work either. Remember my strategy for how to declutter without making a bigger mess? Remember how you got excited because making a bigger mess every time you declutter is your biggest frustration with decluttering? Keep Piles equal a bigger mess in my home. If I make piles and a distraction happens, the piles morph (and grow) while I'm gone. I've made a bigger mess, outside the space I was originally decluttering. If I take things where they go immediately, whenever I get distracted, I've made progress.

Decluttering Question #2: If I Needed This Item, Would It Ever Occur to Me That I Already Had One?

If there's no answer for question #1, ask question #2.

I know I have ponytail holders. I know I have pliers. But I may or may not know that I have a set of glittery nail polishes that I got for Christmas and then left on the fireplace hearth where they were eventually buried under a pile of things like ponytail holders and pliers and trash.

If I didn't even know I had them, they need to go in the Donate Box.

STEP 5: MAKE IT FIT

Trash is gone, things that don't belong in this space are in the places where they do belong, and stuff you wouldn't look for at all is in the Donate Box.

But the room still feels cluttered.

This step is about applying the Container Concept to each area of the room. Surface by surface, shelf by shelf, you're accepting limits of each container and, ultimately, the room.

Are there books shoved every which way on the bookshelf, and maybe, where you can barely see it, a special photo in a special frame turned sideways and pushed to the back?

The books and the photo all passed the "where would I look first?" test.

> Surface by surface, shelf by shelf, you're accepting limits of each container and, ultimately, the room.

But the bookshelf is a container. It is a natural limit that decides how many books you can keep. It's finite. *And it has to also contain that photo.*

If the wonky books shoved on top are wonky because you read them often, they may be your favorites. Pull out your least favorites until all the books *and* the framed photo have space. Real (vertical and everything) space in the container.

I know you're mad right now. I'm using books as my first example. Books are the most emotional of all clutter for so many people like me who'd prefer to live in a fantasy world over the real one.

Fine. I'll talk about other things and come back to books.

Maybe you folded up a bunch of cozy lap blankets during step 2. Folding blankets is easy. You put them in the cute basket you bought on sale because it was perfect for storing blankets. Putting them in the basket was easy, but they've already fallen over because you piled them so high they couldn't balance. Pull out your least favorite blankets until the ones left fit easily in this established blanket-storing space. Without teetering. Put the least favorite blankets in your Donate Box.

Now let's go back to books.

I understand emotions over books, and I get attachment and sentimentality too.

But, y'all, I had to eliminate emotions from my decluttering process. If I let emotions guide me, either good emotions or bad ones, I spiraled down a winding path of crazy. And I didn't get much decluttering done.

I let the container make the tough decisions. I don't have to evaluate the worthiness of each book and somehow worry about offending these inanimate objects. I just have to let the shelf determine how many I can keep.

But let's talk a little more about that framed photo. The one you hadn't seen in a while because it's been shoved sideways or knocked over. If the photo is going to stay there, it needs space. And not just barely enough space to squeeze onto the shelf, but space to do its job.

My definition of clutter is anything that consistently gets out of control. If you only give that photo enough room to stand up, it's going to get squeezed out and knocked over again every time you take out or put back a book. If that happens, something on that shelf (either the photo or some books) are clutter, and they need to go.

But what about the intense desire to go bookshelf shopping so you can keep *all the books*?

This is a living area, right? It's for living. There needs to be room for living. For sitting. For reading. For talking, for plopping down on the couch, for resting together as a family. This means the goal of this room isn't to fit as many books as possible. It's not a storage room or even a library. If another bookshelf would make living more difficult, don't do it.

Once you finish the bookshelf, move on to the next visible pile or space, and work through the steps again. After every out-in-the-open space in this room has been decluttered, you have two choices. Either you can start going through the steps on a nonvisible space in this room (like the drawers of the TV cabinet), or you can move on to the next room's out-in-the-open surfaces. Neither way is wrong. But whatever you choose to do next, look around now and see the difference you've made in this room. Aren't you impressed with yourself?

PAPER CLUTTER

Paper. Paper piles and boxes full of paper and the never-ending influx of paper coming into your mailbox.

Ugh.

I didn't want to include a section on this subject, but since it's *the* question I get more than any other, I'm not sure how I can avoid it. I'm putting it in the chapter about living areas because if paper clutter is an issue for you, it can be an issue in any or every area of your house.

I remind you that this is a book about decluttering and not (as I've said again and again) a book about organizing. I won't tell you how to set up a file cabinet. But I will share strategies I've used in my home over the past eight years that have significantly reduced my paper clutter.

"Less" and "Better"

If you are overrun with paper, you're overwhelmed. Just like any pile of clutter, a pile of paper seems to be a pile of decisions to be made, and paper decisions are the most overwhelming.

But the same strategies that work with any kind of clutter work with paper clutter too.

Get into the mind-set that your goals are "less" and "better"— that anything you can do to reduce the overall mass of paper clutter in your home will be worth the effort. Giving yourself permission to do something without the pressure of solving this never-ending problem once and for all is giving yourself permission to get started.

Just Declutter

Here's a guess: if paper is stressing you out, it's because you have a pile (or sixty-seven piles) somewhere. Here's another guess: you don't need every single piece of paper in those piles. Give yourself permission to just declutter.

And just declutter the easy stuff. The trash and the *Duh*s.

Because important stuff is often made of paper, the brain (at least *my* brain) assumes everything in a paper pile is important. Even when I know that isn't true, I'm so scared to look.

Always look.

When a paper pile overwhelms me and I find myself pretending it doesn't exist, I give myself permission to simply look. To feel absolutely no obligation to make any decisions at all. Just to look at each piece of paper in the pile and only get rid of the ones that are easy.

Every single time I do this, I reduce the pile by more than half.

A smaller pile is less overwhelming. My brain also knows, for a fact, what's in that pile, and I find that I'm more willing and able to deal with it after that knowledge has processed in my brain, even subconsciously, for a while.

Eliminate Procrastination Stations

Paper keeps coming into the house. And keeps coming and keeps coming. The number one thing I have done to dramatically reduce the paper clutter in our home is to walk straight from the mailbox to the trash can (or recycle bin, if you have one) and immediately throw away anything we don't need.

Immediately. Right away. Without stopping.

When I do this, paper stays under control. When I don't, it grows into overwhelming piles. And honestly, I have to be the one to get the mail. While getting the mail sounds like a great job for a kid, it's not. I'm the one who can tell at a glance what needs to go and what needs to stay. If anyone else brings in the mail, it goes straight onto the dining room table, where it grows into a pile of things that might or might not be important.

If you need to shred things that come in daily, walk straight to the shredder as you bring in the mail. One day's shredding won't jam and overheat your shredder the way a year's worth does.

Go Digital

We don't get as much mail as we once did because we receive most of our monthly statements and pay our bills online. We were scared about paying bills online, but now that we do, we absolutely love not having all that paper come into our home. If you're scared, talk to your bank. Most banks so desperately want you to do your banking online that they will help you set up your online account and train you to use it.

Every time you receive a piece of mail that *isn't* trash, check at the bottom of your statement to see if there is a website where you can sign up to go paperless. Do this while you're paying your bills. Gradually, you'll have less paper clutter.

Contain It

You knew I was going to say this, right? The Container Concept works. But if you are overrun with paper, you need to declutter before you contain. Obviously, important papers need to be kept. But if you have piles and piles and boxes and boxes of paper clutter, don't start by heading out to buy a truckload of extra-large filing cabinets. Declutter first. Go through every pile, eliminating the papers you don't need.

By the time you're done, you'll have a better understanding of the type and size of container you need.

But if, by chance, you're not convinced you'll be the best at filing each and every piece of paper the minute it comes into your house (like I'm not), still get a container. Or if you try and fail (like I did), still get a container. I have a plastic, paper-sized container that fits on that piece of countertop in my kitchen where meaningful papers end up anyway.

Meaningful papers go in that container. When it gets full, my brain usually recognizes that I need to go through it and get rid of things that were once meaningful (or I once thought were meaningful) but are no longer meaningful.

Kids' Drawings

The good news is that as your kids grow, they will bring home fewer and fewer keep-worthy papers. That's also the bad news for mamas who dread the end of childhood.

Again, contain it. Get a container for each child. Choose a container that will fit in a space you have to give. (Your container.) Fill up that container, and once it's full, practice the One-In-One-Out Rule.

I know that's simple, but it works.

I promise, if you train your kids to take nonemotional paper straight to the recycle bin, over time they'll identify more and more as nonemotional. Our weekly folder checks for the still-in-elementary child go like this: "Yay! So good, sweetie! Now go throw it away." And neither of us cries.

MORE USEFUL TIPS FOR LIVING AREAS

If you need to move (or remove) furniture, place a shiny gift bag (you know you have extras) under each leg of the piece of furniture. These act as sliders and will help the furniture glide more easily across the floor. Go for minimalism. Identify the essentials needed to help this room serve its purpose. For us, that's super comfortable seating for five and decently comfortable seating for eight. And a TV we can all see from any of those seats. Anything else has to prove itself worthy of being in this room.

ENJOY THE PERKS OF YOUR DECLUTTERED LIVING AREAS

Living areas are on the top of the priority list because they're visible. The visible progress you make in them will increase your energy to keep making progress. But clutter-free living areas also make living easier in general. When living areas are under control, the entire house feels more under control, and you can open the front door without having a panic attack. Yay for fewer clutter-related panic attacks.

KITCHEN

Living areas were first because those are natural gathering areas. Kitchens are almost equally guaranteed to be seen by guests. People wander into the kitchen to help or just to hang out. It's a fact.

It's also a fact that the kitchen needs to look clean. Guests want to know their food is coming from a place they can trust. A decluttered kitchen looks cleaner and is easier to keep clean.

Again, let's work through the steps to tackling an overwhelming mess. Keep the Visibility Rule in mind, starting with visible surfaces first.

STEP 1: TRASH

A bread bag with only a heel. The pasta box that has been empty since last night (or last week) but is still sitting on the counter. Empty boxes of cereal on the breakfast table.

STEP 2: EASY STUFF

Put things away in their established, decision-free homes. Doing easy stuff requires movement but not brain power. In our kitchen there are always random easy things, like an ice chest that's been sitting in the corner of the kitchen since last summer's day at the lake. It needs to go to the garage. That's easy.

The lamp that's sitting on the breakfast table because it seemed easier to bring it in here from the living room than to change the bulb on the kitchen ceiling fan? That's easy. Put a new lightbulb in the ceiling fan and move the lamp back to the living room.

Once the obviously easy stuff is done, it's time to talk about stuff that's easy but completely unfun.

The kitchen has some unique challenges in the easy stuff step. A lot of the easy stuff in the kitchen is procrasticlutter, and procrasticlutter is procrasticlutter because you don't love doing it. Irritation over the existence of procrasticlutter can make easy stuff feel like it's not easy.

Example: dirty dishes. Dirty dishes require an additional step before they get put away. They have to be washed. There's no decision to make about whether dishes need to be washed, and that makes them easy. Even though stopping this decluttering project to wash dishes feels wrong, do it. There is no way around this.

But here's a decluttering clue for later that should make you feel better: you like your dirty dishes more than you like the clean ones sitting in the cabinets.

Those dishes are dirty because you chose them. They're dirty while others are clean because you chose them *over* the dishes that are sitting in your cabinets.

(If every dish you own is dirty, don't be discouraged. You just need my other book, *How to Manage Your Home Without Losing Your Mind*.)

STEP 3: *DUH* CLUTTER

As your dishwasher is running or dishes are drying on the counter, look for *Duh* donations on surfaces and inside cabinets and drawers.

I know. I just went against my own Visibility Rule and it's only the second room. In the kitchen, multiple items, large and small, get pulled out of and put back into drawers and cabinets every day, so function is everything. Decluttering both visible surfaces and inside closed cabinets is important.

Without pulling everything out, look for obvious clutter that can go straight in the Donate Box. *Duh*s might be a weird-sized bonus skillet from a set of pots and pans. Maybe it's the bag of canned goods you put together to donate but then never did. Stick those in the Donate Box.

The goal here, as always, is to reduce the overall volume of stuff. Reducing the volume of stuff reduces the visible scariness of the task and helps you gain momentum in this room.

STEP 4: ASK THE DECLUTTERING QUESTIONS

You've cleared the easy stuff. Now it's time to dig into piles and drawers and cabinets. Start with any piles that exist out in the open, and go through the steps, one mess at a time.

Decluttering Question #1: If I Needed This Item, Where Would I Look for It First?

You're asking yourself where you'd look first if the counter were clear. (The counter being clear is the goal, right?) Wherever you'd look first, take it there now.

If you hem and haw at decluttering question #1, ask yourself the second decluttering question.

Decluttering Question #2: If I Needed This Item, Would It Ever Occur to Me That I Already Had One?

For example, a garlic press. If you needed to mince garlic, would you search for your garlic press? Or would you smash the garlic with the side of the knife you were using to chop other vegetables?

Would you do this without ever stopping to consider if you have a garlic press?

In the kitchen, question #2 isn't always a matter of whether I would go out and buy the item; it's a matter of whether my natural inclination would be to make do with another kitchen tool that has lots of different uses and works perfectly fine for this job too.

> **The decluttering questions work because they deal with reality only. Not possibilities, potential, or emotion.**

What I can't do is hold a garlic press in my hand and ponder whether it's a valuable and useful item. Of course it is! *But I don't use it*. The decluttering questions work because they deal with reality only. Not possibilities, potential, or emotion.

Yay for simple questions that make decisions simple.

By the time your surfaces (other than the ones where dishes lay drying) are clear and you've removed all the stuff you don't like (or know for a fact you don't use) from the drawers and cabinets, your dishes will hopefully be dry.

STEP 5: MAKE IT FIT

As you put away clean dishes, the Container Concept will slap you in the face. View your plate shelf as a container. The size of that shelf (or those shelves) determines how many plates you can keep. And they have to fit comfortably. (Comfortably means not squeezed in so tight you have to rearrange the cabinet every time you need a plate.)

Remember: The dishes you just washed are your favorites. You chose them over the dishes that are left in the cabinet. They deserve cabinet space more than the ones sitting in there that you don't use as often.

Step 5.1: Consolidate

In my kitchen, things are mostly already consolidated. I have a coffee cup shelf and a utensil drawer. But if you're struggling to accept the limitations of your container, consciously consolidate.

Put pasta pots together. Stack skillets. Put all your saucepans in one place.

If you can't fit your favorite pasta pot (that you just washed) comfortably in the cabinet, count how many pasta pots you have. Two? Seven? This one is your favorite, so start removing your least favorite(s) until it fits.

If there isn't room for the two skillets you need to put away, and you truly use both skillets regularly, remove one (or two) more of those pasta pots to make room.

Keep consolidating. Don't worry, we're not getting organized. This is still decluttering. Organizing would be pot racks and shelf dividers and such, and we're not going there. But consolidating is part of decluttering.

Consolidating is a reality check.

I remember exactly what I wore for my school awards assembly back in 1989, but I have absolutely no idea how many pots or pans I have unless I'm looking in my pots-and-pans cabinet.

And if I can't see one pan because it's hidden behind another pot, it simply doesn't exist in my universe.

Consolidating breaks through that mental block for me. To consolidate, I have to actively move things. Consciously look at things. What was a "decent number of skillets" becomes five skillets. The number five (a concrete number as opposed to my totally ambiguous concept of how many I might have) registers in my brain as more than I need. And as that realization hits me, my eyes are opened, and the three I rarely use (and don't actually like) reveal themselves to me.

Step 5.2: Purge Down to the Limits of the Container

Keep going. Declutter until the things that are left fit comfortably in the space you have and are easily accessible. Leave space to reach in and grab the skillet you need without first having to move your slow cooker out of the way.

THE PANTRY

A kitchen is so much more than pots and pans and silverware. It's food too. If you don't have a pantry, use these steps wherever you store your shelf-stable foods or spices.

Step 1: Trash

In the pantry, trash is expired stuff. (If you want to argue about that, wait until the end of this chapter.) Trash is empty boxes and bags, and almost empty boxes and bags with a small amount of stale food in them.

Step 2: Easy Stuff

Like everywhere else, easy stuff in the pantry is the stuff that has an already established home somewhere else in the house. Like a stuffed animal. Or a tube of toothpaste. *It happens.*

Take these things to their homes.

Step 3: *Duh* Clutter

Start pulling out *Duh*s. In the pantry, *Duh*s are the things you will never eat. It happens to me too. I buy something because it's *such* a great deal, or my mom sends me home after Memorial Day with a bag full of cookies and canned goods, and most of it is still sitting in my pantry on the Fourth of July (of the following year). Or I thought for sure I was going to love a new recipe and bought two of something (because there was a buy-one-get-one-free sale), but we hated the recipe, and I'd never use the odd ingredient for anything else.

In an ideal world these things would leave my pantry gradually as I notice they're there and realize I'll never use them. But I don't live in an ideal world. I live in my house. In my house, I need focused decluttering time to deal with these things.

Off to the Donate Box they go.

Step 4: Ask the Decluttering Questions

Work through the two decluttering questions. In the pantry, I like to think I only have things I'd actually look for in there. But asking myself these questions helps me realize that even though I had a moment when I thought the pantry was a great place to stick my tortilla warmer, I wouldn't actually look for it there.

Step 5: Make It Fit

I always felt sorry for myself over my lack of proper pantry space. By *proper*, I mean bigger than what I had.

I pouted because I couldn't fit new groceries into my existing shelves, but I was wrong. Those existing shelves held full-sized boxes with only one cracker inside. Or expired food. Or were just so scattered and whompyjawed that the stuff inside took up twice the room it would need if it were neatly arranged.

If your pantry was crazy before you started this process, my guess is that you now have a lot more available space in there than you thought you would. I assume that removing easy stuff has freed up quite a bit of room.

Step 5.1: Consolidate

Put rice together, pasta together, and jars of sauces together. If there's a single serving of dried pinto beans in the bottoms of four different bags, combine them into one. Canned goods go in one place, grouped according to what's in each can.

Remember, consolidating is my reality check. This simple step shows me if I've been grabbing one box of angel-hair pasta every time I've been to the store for the past two months. Usually, though not always, this realization helps me *not* grab it the next time.

Step 5.2: Purge Down to the Limits of the Container

Before we focus on getting this purged down to fit the space, do one last reality check. Look around your kitchen (or in the trunk of your car) for any random pantry items that were never put away. Put them away. If your new stuff still won't fit, let me tell you a secret: it won't fit.

This is the Container Concept. The size of the pantry space you have is the size of the pantry space you have.

But don't use the fact that it doesn't all fit as a reason to start shopping for a new house. Use it as a reason to keep decluttering. If there's only so much space available for canned goods, that space is full of canned goods, and you have a sack full of canned goods that needs to be put away, use the One-In-One-Out Rule. For every can that needs to go into the pantry, remove a less desirable can to make room.

This motivates me to be realistic. I love red beans and rice, but I make it once a year at the most. I need only two cans to make that one meal. If I bought two cans because I mistakenly thought I didn't have any, they don't need to go in the pantry too. I put the older (but not expired) two cans in the Donate Box. Eventually, if I kept them, I would use all four cans. *But I don't have room for four cans.*

If I need to put away four cans of peas, but see I already have twelve cans of peas, I learn I tend to pick up peas regularly. Twelve is (more than) enough, so I stick the four oldest (but not expired) cans in the Donate Box.

I don't have to evaluate the nutritional value of each item; I just have to acknowledge that the size of my cabinet determines how much I can keep in my home at one time.

Maybe I found barbecue sauce in that grocery bag that was sitting on the kitchen floor. I need barbecue sauce, but I don't have space for it because the pantry is already full.

So I look in the pantry for something I don't need as badly as I need that barbecue sauce. I find a jar of artichokes. I love artichokes, but I love the ones from the can. The jar? Not so much. Too pickly.

I justified keeping them earlier because I truly might use them someday. But I need a space for barbecue sauce that I'll definitely use, so I am free to stick the jar of artichokes into the Donate Box. I don't even feel guilty. I'm not insulting the artichokes. I'm just facing reality. Stuff we will definitely eat deserves shelf space more than stuff we might never eat.

THE FRIDGE

I'm going to divide the fridge into two parts: the inside and the outside.

I'll devote a few words to the outside: look at each thing hanging on it, throw away anything irrelevant (expired coupons, school notes from last year, and so on), and stick magnets you don't like in the Donate Box.

Now marvel at how much better your entire kitchen looks since the eyesore you never noticed is no longer an eyesore.

Now, the inside of the fridge. Ugh.

I hate this part, but let's break it down.

Step 1: Trash

I drag my trash can in front of the fridge and start dumping. Empty jelly jars. A bottle of olives with a single olive in it, sitting next to the new olives. Empty milk jugs. *Don't ask.*

Random stuff I wouldn't eat even if my life depended on eating something. Take out containers. Ziploc bags that hold three leftover tater tots I totally thought I would eat with my lunch the next day, but "the next day" was more than a month ago.

You get the picture, so I'll move on.

Step 2: Easy Stuff

Stuff that has a home other than the fridge, but for some strange reason is in the fridge, is easy. There's always something. I usually find hot pads or serving utensils in there.

Unfortunately, reusable containers that need to be emptied of their contents, whether those contents are still identifiable or not, are easy. Cleaning them out isn't the least bit fun, but there's no decision to be made.

Step 3: *Duh* Clutter

This is the "Why Do I Have This?" stuff like the odd-sounding marinade that came in a gift basket last Christmas. It's the fat-free salad dressing you thought was going to help you lose twelve pounds but turned out to be disgusting.

Step 4: Ask the Decluttering Questions

There may or may not be an opportunity to use the first decluttering question in the fridge, but you have it if you need it.

The second decluttering question, however, is useful: If I needed this item, would it ever occur to me that I already had one?

With food, this happens to me a lot. I have no idea I already have one in the fridge, so I buy another while I'm at the store. Sometimes this conscious cleaning out will help me remember to use it, but sometimes I have to admit I am never going to eat it. If thinking about this makes your head want to explode, don't worry. I'll dive more into the dilemma of food waste soon.

Step 5: Make It Fit

This one is easier in the fridge than in the pantry, because there probably (hopefully) aren't any groceries waiting to go into the fridge sitting in a bag on the floor. If your fridge is still overfull after the first three steps to working through the mess, contain. Make it fit. Accept that the size of your fridge is the size of your fridge.

When I lived in Thailand, we had a small fridge. It was slightly bigger than the dorm fridges I had in college but significantly smaller than the smallest fridge I've had at any other time in my adult life. And the freezer was tiny.

And you know what? My fridge was the size it was. So profound, right? *Even after the fiftieth time I've said a version of that statement.*

I can't completely compare because I wasn't feeding a family of five at that time, but we survived. My roommates and I cooked almost every evening at home and kept snacks and breakfast foods in that fridge. Our reality was that we had a small fridge, and we made that reality work.

I remind myself that one of my reasons for thinking I need a humongous fridge is cultural. A giant refrigerator is normal in my part of the world. But the main reason I once thought I needed an even bigger fridge was that I had too much stuff in the one I had.

Step 5.1: Consolidate

Start putting like things together. Again, this will reveal ridiculous multiples that may have escaped your notice when you were pulling out trash and obvious stuff.

It also might free you to get rid of the almost empty ketchup if you realize you have four almost full bottles. You'll realize you never got rid of that strange-tasting salsa even after you brought home the kind everyone likes.

Step 5.2: Purge Down to the Limits of the Container

Honestly, this step is rarely needed for me when I'm cleaning out (decluttering) my fridge. Getting rid of easy stuff and revealing excessive multiples through consolidating usually leaves lots of space. But if you still need to purge, apply what you've learned so far, and get rid of enough stuff that the things left can be accessed easily.

Now your counters and your pantry and your fridge are so much better off than they were when you started. Your kitchen, overall, feels significantly more functional than it did yesterday. Enjoy it. But if certain kitchen-clutter-related questions still plague your soul, don't skip the next chapter.

Chapter 13

ANOTHER CHAPTER ABOUT KITCHENS

Kitchens have a lot of challenges, and I have a lot to say about those challenges. I have so much to say that my editor thought it needed to be two chapters instead of one really, really long one. In this chapter I cover specific issues and specific mind-set changes that will have a major impact on your kitchen.

THE FOOD STORAGE CONTAINER CABINET

I won't address each and every issue that could possibly come up in every space in every home. You will have to take the things you learn and apply them to your unique home and unique clutter.

But while I'm leaving it to you to apply "pantry" principles to your baking supplies and go through the same steps in the silverware drawer that you used in the dinner plate cabinet, I am going to talk specifically about the cabinet where you keep food storage containers.

This is some of the most direct, I-don't-care-about-your-unique-situation-this-is-what-works advice I will give anywhere in this book.

Store food storage containers with their lids on.

I'm telling you: this works.

You bought a book about decluttering. I told you my goal was not perfection but *less*. Not magazine-worthy after photos but spaces that fit your lifestyle and stay under control with minimal mental anguish.

If you had to hold your nose and stifle your gag reflex as you opened up food storage containers full of unidentifiable inedibles, you have too many food storage containers. You most definitely have too many if you have a sink full of soaking-in-bleach-water containers that came out of the fridge *and* you have clean ones in your cabinet.

The issue is limiting your number of food storage containers to the "container" available, which is the cabinet where you keep them.

Everyone knows you can fit more food storage containers into a cabinet if you nest them. Especially if you get the kind that all use the same size lids and vary only by height so they can *all* nest.

But the goal isn't to get as many into the available space as possible.

It's to declutter. To make the space easy to use and able to stay under control pretty much all the time.

Here's my problem with stuffing in as many containers as possible: If I grab a container for my leftover spaghetti, I can't just grab the container. I have to get the right-sized container out of the middle of the neat little nesting stack. And now this means I have two (or more, depending on whether I got the right size on the first try) stacks of nested container-bottoms that need to be re-nested.

And I knock over the neat little stack of lids, even though I was just grabbing the one off the top. Or I pull out one lid from the cool lid-storing gadget thingy and send the rest toppling to the floor.

I just wanted to put my spaghetti in the fridge. *I do not have time to reorganize the entire blankety-blank cabinet.*

And every time I put the containers away, there's arranging

involved. And thinking involved. And more-than-minimal effort involved. So honestly, I used to (literally) shove lids and bottoms into the cabinet as quickly as possible so I could slam the door shut and hopefully avoid the avalanche.

That didn't work. The cabinet was a huge mess at all times.

I came up with a system that isn't the least bit complicated but totally works: I put lids on containers as I take them out of the dishwasher (or off the dish drainer when I hand wash) and stick them in the cabinet.

They don't nest, so no finagling is required.

When I need a container, I grab it. All of it. No searching for a matching lid.

It's truly one of the best and most lasting solutions I've come up with.

I can't keep as many (anywhere near as many), but that's okay. I didn't need as many as I once believed I needed.

Remember all those gross ones in the fridge? My fridge was an endless and infinite black hole. I had no idea how many containers were shoved in the back of the fridge until I ran out of clean storage containers.

When my goal was to get as many as I possibly could into the space I had, I had a bazillion. I could go longer before I had to clean out the fridge, losing meatballs and macaroni and giving mango chunks time to shape-shift into something very different from, and way scarier than, mango.

A smaller number of containers meant I was more aware we were running out, and I cleaned out the fridge more often. This meant we wasted less food. And we didn't suffer injuries from falling containers when I opened the cabinet door. And I didn't lose my mind when I could find every size lid except the one that matched the container I had just filled with food.

That's a triple win.

WASTING FOOD

I mentioned wasted food. Let's talk about that. I've been planning to bring it up since we talked about the pantry, which is probably when you thought about it. You might have thought bad thoughts about me for telling you to throw away ~~perfectly~~ probably good food. I generally get bothered by such things too. But this is a book about decluttering. (Are you tired of me saying that yet?)

The goal is to make your home easier to manage. An easier-to-manage home will mean less wasted food in the future. Get that? *Less wasted food is the goal.*

But you're not living in your Goal World yet. The real question is: Have you already wasted the food?

I am not here to debate whether dates stamped on packages are sell-by dates or you'll-probably-die-if-you-eat-this dates.

That isn't the issue. The issue is that you haven't eaten it, and it has expired. If you aren't willing to let the printed expiration dates be your deciding decluttering factor, consider these things:

If you purchased the food after it expired because you're fanatical about saving money, great. But you need to eat it soon, *because it was already expired when you bought it.*

If you bought it in a normal grocery store at a normal distance from its expiration date, ask yourself: Why haven't I eaten it yet? Do I not actually like it? Did it get lost behind a mass of other cans and boxes? That's why you're decluttering. You don't want to lose things anymore.

You have three choices: You can eat it tonight. You can throw it away. Or . . . you can donate food that isn't expired so there's room to keep the expired stuff.

Note: You can't donate expired food. Really. Food banks have to throw it out, so that wastes everyone's time. If you're the one convinced it's okay to eat expired food, then you need to be the one to eat it.

The goal here is to live in the real world. *Your* real world. The world where you do or do not eat expired food.

I'm an idealist too. I feel horrible guilt when I have to throw something away that could have fed a child in my community if I had either not purchased it in the first place or donated it before it expired.

Even worse, I know from experience how the denial/procrastination cycle goes. I see that something is expired, and I feel guilty for wasting food. But I don't like feeling bad, so I nip that feeling in the bud and stick the expired food back into the cabinet. I tell myself that I've read somewhere that some foods can still

> I have finally embraced Realistic Right-Now Me. She's the one who makes lasting progress in my home.

be eaten for a certain amount of time after the date that's stamped on the can. I just don't know which foods can last how long. I'll have to look that up.

The idea of Future Me being so resourceful (looking things up) and so idealistic (not wasting that long-forgotten can of tuna) makes me feel happy and proud.

I like feeling happy and proud way more than I like feeling guilty.

But idealistic Future Me lives in the future. She exists tomorrow, the day that's always a day away.

I have finally embraced Realistic Right-Now Me. She's the one who makes lasting progress in my home.

Realistic Right-Now Me likes tuna. But she doesn't like the idea of eating tuna that's a little fishy. "Fishy" as in is-this-going-to-be-the-last-tuna-I-ever-eat? Realistic Right-Now Me has to admit that if I don't want to eat the tuna now, I need to get rid of it.

Here are some things to think about while you're deciding whether a certain can of tuna or spinach or garbanzo beans gets to stay.

Can I Eat It Today?

You *just said* it was fine to eat, so eat it. If you're balking at my bossiness, is it because you have an elaborate meal planned for tonight after your long day of pantry decluttering? Okay, then put it on the menu for tomorrow night or a week from today (since you're such an amazing menu-plan maker). Or eat it for lunch tomorrow.

What's that? You have no idea what to do with garbanzo beans? Well, there's this thing called the Internet, and you can look up "fast and easy garbanzo beans recipe." Or just make hummus. Garbanzo beans are the same thing as chickpeas, and if you drain them and blend them with some olive oil and spices, they taste amazing spread on pita bread or dipped with a carrot.

I know we're getting off track here, and I know you are probably experiencing a vague memory of someone casually mentioning garbanzo beans and homemade hummus in a book you read once, and you're pretty sure that's why you have them.

My point is that you need to either eat the garbanzo beans or get rid of them. And no, I have no idea how long garbanzo beans are nonpoisonous after their expiration date. You'll have to search the Internet for that too.

Or you can throw them away.

Throwing away food should hurt. Let the intense feeling of regret change how you shop in the future. As you reach for an unusual ingredient in the store, let the memory of this regrettable moment make you pause. In that pause, you'll either search for "fast and easy garbanzo beans recipe" on your phone (so you can grab any other ingredients you need to make the recipe this week), or you'll put the can back on the shelf (because you don't have the energy to go through all that hassle).

Either way is better than what we have here: possibly edible food and a whole lot of regret.

Have I Ever Passed This Up in Favor of Something Unexpired?

I once had a can of blueberry pie filling. I think I brought it home after a weekend at the lake with extended family. My husband makes amazing pancakes, and I wanted to let people request special fruity ones.

Except that if you are going to make blueberry pancakes, get blueberries. Not blueberry pie filling. It doesn't really work the same.

We learned the hard way with the first can, so the second can came home unopened.

I'd seen that can of blueberry pie filling in the cabinet for a while. I wasn't sure exactly how long it had been there, but we'd been laughing about blueberry pie pancakes for a long time.

Then one day, I needed to make a pie. Blueberry seemed the perfect choice, because I already had blueberry pie filling. But when I went to open the can, I saw that it was expired. *Several years expired.*

And though I hemmed and hawed and told myself my mother would have used it and that we'd all most likely be alive tomorrow, I just couldn't do it. I couldn't handle the thought of ruining our holiday with blueberry-pie poisoning.

So I got in my car, drove to the store, and bought another can of pie filling.

And left the expired blueberry pie filling in the cabinet.

Because, most likely, it was fine. Except that I'd passed it up for something not expired.

Have you ever passed up expired food in favor of something similar that wasn't expired? Did you, like me, pass it up because that day just wasn't a good day to be sick?

As someone who has such bizarre thoughts on a regular basis, allow me to ask you what I've had to ask myself many times: *Um, hello? And when exactly is it a good time to be sick?*

If you believe expired food is good enough to eat, then eat it. If you hesitate to eat it, throw it out.

I'm sorry. I really am, because I know how much it hurts to give up on how resourceful idealistic Future Me was going to be. Robbing her of the opportunity to prove her creativity and frugality feels downright cruel.

But remember your goal: a house that's easier to manage because it doesn't hold stuff you are never going to use.

And you aren't going to use food you're not willing to eat.

REPURPOSING

Are you a repurposer? Yay! That's awesome!

Or are you a *wanna-be* repurposer?

There's a big difference. I was somewhere in between. I collected stuff like I was the world's greatest reuser of all things that looked like trash to the untrained eye.

In every pickle jar or childproof medicine container, I saw not only dill slices or pills; I saw the future.

I saw baking soda being stored in a perfectly good (and *free*) glass container, and I saw tiny beads sorted neatly by color.

Creativity is awesome, and I love the side of me that sees the world differently. I celebrate her.

But I have to reconcile her with the other side of me. The other side of me is perfectly fine living in clutter—until I'm not. Until I'm late for an important appointment or awaiting the ring of a doorbell, and I can't find what I need or I have nowhere to shove things because an entire cabinet (and maybe more) is full of trash.

Trash with possibilities, but still trash.

And then I despise Creative Me.

The number one way I've found to keep this precarious balance in check is to declutter. Every time I cleaned out a cabinet full of empty spaghetti-sauce jars, I viewed each new spaghetti-sauce jar that entered my home differently.

Decluttering Question #1 applies here too. Where would I look for it first? Honestly, on the rare occasion I needed an empty pickle jar, I'd change my meal plan for the day so I could empty the jar that was in the fridge and use it immediately. Usually, I wouldn't even remember I had a stash of empty pickle jars in the cabinet. (Hello, Decluttering Question #2!)

I forgot about my collection because these were *everyday* items that were constantly coming into my home.

Employ the decluttering strategy of using things. While I decluttered my kitchen, I stopped to transfer baking powder and cornstarch into a couple of the glass containers. That used two, and I immediately saw the twenty that were left in the cabinet as clutter. I stuck those in the Donate Box. (Or you can put them in the trash bag or the recycling bin.)

If your heart's desire is to be prepared for projects and crafts in the future, go ahead and keep empty ketchup bottles—if you have the space to store them. Just let that space limit the number you keep.

As you come across better, more useful jars and bottles, use the One-In-One-Out Rule.

THE HEAD EXPLOSION RULE

Before I finish this second chapter about kitchens, let me point out that you will likely find opportunities to make use of my Head Explosion Rule while you're decluttering your kitchen.

I created the Head Explosion Rule for but-but-but situations.

I apply this rule if the two decluttering questions are too overwhelming. I use it when I can't clear the mental image of myself as a world saver and frugal queen. If I feel like my head is going to explode over a decision that isn't life changing, but feels totally life changing, I choose to declutter the item.

Because no item is worth my head exploding.

GRANDMA'S DISHES

I've talked about plates, pots, pans, and pickle jars. You've realized the dishes you actually use are your favorites.

But what about Grandma's dishes? Or Aunt Sally's crocheted potholders? Or Uncle Henry's hand-carved cutting board?

Even though they're special and legitimately sentimental, the Container Concept still applies.

Do they fit in the container that is your kitchen? If you don't use them, are they taking up container space that is needed for things you do use?

Ultimately, every question comes down to the Container Concept. Do you have the space to keep these things? If not, what are you willing to get rid of so you can keep them?

Honestly, the kitchen is such an intensely used space in the home (things moving in and out of cabinets and drawers on a multiple-times-each-day basis) that I don't consider my kitchen to be a place to store things I will never actually use.

It's your decision, but here are some things to consider: Are you keeping these things because you love them, or because you feel guilty about not keeping them? Can you use them?

Aunt Sally didn't crochet those potholders so you would stick them in a drawer and think ugly thoughts about them every time you felt frustrated over the state of your kitchen. She crocheted them so people she loved would be able to protect their dining room tables from the scorching heat of freshly cooked meals. Using items like these, sometimes to the point where they get completely used up, brings about a tiny bit of the feeling I have when a loved one passes away after a long and full life. I'm sad, and the grief is real. But I feel no regret because the items did what they were created to do. They fulfilled their purpose.

Treasure, don't store. If Uncle Henry loved carving so much that he never considered how much bacteria would collect in the lines of his design, do you love this cutting board enough to use it as a decoration? Can you hang it on the wall where it makes you smile? That's a much better option than grumbling every time you have to dig around in a too-full cabinet to find a cutting board you can actually use.

If there's an entire collection of Grandma's plates that you don't love and aren't willing to make space for by getting rid of the ones you actually use, can you keep one? A plate hanging on the wall will remind you of her every day. She'd like that better than a messy kitchen anyway.

BEDROOMS

My favorite thing about bedrooms is how you can close the doors and hope no one opens them during a party.

Sort of kidding.

Sort of not.

We've tackled living areas (super visible) and kitchens (very visible). Now we're ready for bedrooms (not visible if I can possibly help it).

Here's the thing: if you've worked to declutter your living areas and kitchen, and have been going back to re-declutter them when you have some time (so they stay decluttered), you may just be ready to get to bedrooms on that prioritizing-by-visibility scale.

And a decluttered bedroom is like candy. Having a floor I can walk across in the dark without tripping thrills my soul.

My biggest complaint, though, about decluttering a bedroom is how quickly it gets re-cluttered.

Before I started my deslobification process, the lightning-fast re-cluttering made me question the point of working in my bedroom. But every time I re-declutter a bedroom (not reorganize, but re-*declutter*), it stays under control a little longer. And I'm willing to get rid of a little more than I could bear to declutter last time.

So getting started, no matter how overwhelming, is worth your time.

HOW I STARTED MAKING LASTING
PROGRESS IN MY BEDROOM

I stopped (or mostly stopped) Stuff Shifting.

My bedroom finally started staying under control for longer periods of time when I decluttered my living areas and kitchen and defined the purposes of those rooms. As I removed their clutter from my home, my bedroom was easier to maintain as well.

I Stuff Shifted for years, even though I called it *decluttering*. I moved things from one area to another, assuming the problem was that I hadn't found the right way to store it, not that I had too much. When a moment of panic happened (because someone was coming over), I moved all homeless items to the bedroom to get them out of the way. The master bedroom was my dumping ground.

Here's what I'm *not* going to tell you: a bedroom should be a sanctuary, a place of peace and rest and blah, blah, blah.

Not that that isn't true. It's totally true. But knowing it was true wasn't the least bit helpful in my own quest for a clutter-free bedroom. My bedroom was the most overwhelming space in my home. The storage room I never realized was a storage room, but was totally a storage room.

If that's you, and you're feeling angsty because you're just not ready to face your bedroom, don't. Wait. Move on to another space in your home, or focus on the closet in the master bedroom (closets get their own chapter soon). It's okay. Really.

We could get all psycho-babbly and talk about how I was putting myself last in my own home and that was why my own sleeping space (and, sadly, my collaterally damaged husband's sleeping space) was not a priority.

Or we could just admit that it was the easiest room to put off dealing with.

Whatever. If you're ready to dive in, let's go.

Grab a black trash bag and a Donate Box.

It's the same thing every time. But please don't reinvent the wheel in this room. Of all the rooms in my home, my own bedroom sent my brain firing off in all different directions. Before I established this process, I found myself doing a little here and a little there and then spending five hours alphabetizing my husband's CD collection.

The stuff in my bedroom was totally random. My efforts were completely random. But once I applied the strategies I'd developed in other overwhelming (but less overwhelming than this) spaces of my home, I finally made progress.

STEP 1: TRASH

Start with trash. Trash is the easiest of the easy stuff. Throw things away. Stacks of random unimportant papers. Empty deodorant containers. Tissue that missed the trash can last time you had a ferocious allergy attack. Empty tissue boxes.

Don't worry about digging and moving and sorting everything in every pile (yet). Just grab the obvious trash.

STEP 2: EASY STUFF

For a bedroom that's a dumping ground, this step is overwhelming. Don't let it be. When I say to do the easy stuff, I'm talking about the so-ridiculously-obvious-that-it-isn't-obvious-anymore stuff.

Like clothes on the floor.

Don't get organized. We're not changing your ways or implementing long-term solutions today. Decluttering clothing is another chapter. Just pick up the clothes and start filling your laundry hamper or laundry basket or put them in a pile. (A single, distinct pile.)

We're still on step 2, but as you pick clothing up off the floor, you're going to find some *Duh* clothing donations. Make a pile of them.

I am generally anti-pile, but this is a pile with a purpose. It's a laundry pile. As in, those *Duh* donations will go straight to your washing machine so you can put them straight into a Donate Box as you pull them out of the dryer.

When I say to do the easy stuff, I'm talking about the so-ridiculously-obvious-that-it-isn't-obvious-anymore stuff.

As a general rule, thrift stores do not wash clothing. You need to wash clothes that have been on the floor and are probably dirty, just like you'd wash them before you'd wear them.

But this isn't the time for perfection or for letting laundry rituals justify procrastination.

Did you know that many, *many* people don't sort laundry by color? Enough people love this method that I decided to try it. It's not my normal laundry strategy, but if I'm doing disaster recovery that involves clothing that needs to be washed before I donate, I wash it all together.

Dump your donation pile in the washing machine, put the setting on normal, add some detergent, and start it running through the cycle.

Now head back to the bedroom.

Keep going with easy stuff. Clothes from the floor go into the dirty clothes bin. Clothes piled on that chair in the corner need to go back onto hangers and into the closet. Same goes for the ones draped over your exercise bike. Clothes are easy.

But let's talk about something that will probably come up at this point in the process, and that you may have already experienced in your efforts to declutter living areas and the kitchen.

What do you do when the place where you'd put something is its own decluttering project that needs to happen? How do you avoid stopping what you were doing, working on *that* space, and getting completely off track?

Remember the Container Concept: any space that holds things is a container. And remember your current project. Right now isn't the time to clear out the closet, so if there truly isn't enough room to simply hang up the dress, practice the One-In-One-Out Rule.

Choose one thing that deserves to be hanging in your closet less than the item you're putting in there. One thing that is less container worthy than the thing in your hand.

The One-In-One-Out Rule does nothing to make the closet better, but the closet isn't what you're working on right now. And the thing you took out of the closet is going straight into the Donate Box that's ready and waiting in the bedroom where you're already decluttering.

Putting anything in the Donate Box or the trash bag is a decluttering win.

Now get back to the easy stuff.

As you clear the floor and surfaces of clothes, you'll likely (in my case, definitely) uncover other things that were hiding under or among the piles of clothes. I once found, early on in my deslobification process, five sticks of deodorant.

If you're finding such things, and you start to feel exasperated with yourself, just keep doing the easy stuff. Berating yourself isn't easy. Taking five sticks of deodorant to the bathroom drawer where you'd look for them first is easy.

Go ahead and do it.

Another thing I find a *lot* of when I excavate a messy bedroom is hangers. Oh my word, the hangers that hide on the floor. Grab them and take them where they go. Y'know, to the closet.

Hangers are a great example of how taking things where they

go immediately doesn't necessarily mean taking them individually. Individually would mean a thousand separate trips, so I look around and grab as many hangers as I can carry, since I'm going to the closet anyway.

Now make another run through the room with the black trash bag. Each layer of clutter that's peeled back reveals more trash. And I know we're spending more time on easy stuff than in most other chapters, but that's the reality of a dumping ground. So many of the individual items are easy. But together, in a big floor-covering pile, they're overwhelming.

Once the floors are generally clear of easy stuff, move on to the bed. Make it. Making the bed is easy. If you're working in this room around the change of a season, remove the out-of-season bedding that's wadded up at the foot of the bed.

STEP 3: *DUH* CLUTTER

Scan the room for *Duh*s. You very likely found some as you worked on the easy stuff, but take a quick and purposeful look around for boxes of outgrown clothes that somehow ended up in this room instead of the trunk of your car. You'll also find that some of the things dumped in here in moments of Stuff Shifting are now easy because your view of clutter has been changing as you've worked on other areas of your home.

Once you've made your way through the top layer of trash, easy stuff, and *Duh*s, start working on individual piles, starting with the most visible ones first.

This is the not-so-easy stuff. The stuff that makes you want to keep pretending this room doesn't exist. If you are sure an individual pile is full of difficult, emotional clutter, look again for trash within that single pile.

I suppose it's possible there is no trash in that pile. But prove it. *Do not assume you know what's in the pile.* Look. Always look.

No matter how convinced I am that I know what is in a pile, I'm wrong 93.792 percent of the time. Always, *always* look.

When I decluttered a cabinet in our game room recently, I was completely confident I knew what was in a large white box decorated with childhood drawings by my (now aged fifty) husband. I *knew* it was filled with penciled drawings of Batman and Robin and various other muscly fighting men. I was confident I'd opened it before and seen exactly that.

I was so sure, I almost didn't open the box.

But then I reminded myself I *have* to look. I can't assume. I pulled off the lid and found . . . a *fourth* chess set. As in, I had already uncovered three other sets during that same decluttering project.

The fourth, y'all. I can justify one chess set, but we won't be organizing a chess tournament any time soon.

No matter what you assume is in that pile, look. When I look, in addition to trash and easy stuff, I often find IBMTs (I've Been Meaning Tos) or WDIHTs (Why Do I Have Thats). Those are *Duh*s. Don't spend energy or emotion on *Duh*s, because plenty of other things will require energy and emotion. Just stick them in the Donate Box.

Get the trash out. Take easy things to their established homes. Put *Duh*s in the Donate Box.

STEP 4: ASK THE DECLUTTERING QUESTIONS

Finally, it's time for the decluttering questions. You can ask them at any point, but I've waited until now because making a visible impact by doing the easy stuff first is key to gaining momentum in a difficult space like this one.

But now you're tackling stacks and piles that aren't easy, so the decluttering questions are essential.

In my bedroom, there's a section of floor space just outside the paths we take to go from the bedroom door to the bed to the master bathroom and closets. That rarely trodden section of floor attracts things that aren't easy, things that don't have an established home. Clearing that space of clutter makes a shocking impact on the overall room. A clear floor makes a room not look wackadoodle. That spurs me to keep going.

So item by item in that space, and then working through other visible piles, I ask the decluttering questions.

Decluttering Question #1: If I Needed This Item, Where Would I Look for It First?

No analysis, no angst, no deep thinking allowed. Just follow your instinct and take it there. If you don't have an instinctive answer to give, ask question #2.

Decluttering Question #2: If I Needed This Item, Would It Ever Occur to Me That I Already Had One?

If not, it goes in the Donate Box.

Ask these questions until the pile is gone. Move to the next visible pile and continue working your way through the entire room's visible spaces.

STEP 5: MAKE IT FIT

Once you've eliminated the piles of randomness, it's time to talk containers. A big part of seeing the room as a container is defining the purpose of the room.

A bedroom is for sleeping. It needs to hold a bed, and the bed needs to be easily accessible. Stacks of books creating a maze that leads to the bed aren't okay. This is a bedroom.

But a bedroom is also referred to as *so-and-so's room*. My husband's and my room is *our room*. My sons' room is *the boys' room*, and my daughter has a room. Other areas of the home are communal, but bedrooms are where individuals keep personal treasures.

Designating spaces within the room for personal treasures goes far in keeping a bedroom under control. I have a table where I keep book-writing stuff that needs to not be subject to the rest of the house. My husband has a cabinet for his music collection. My sons have certain drawers that are theirs to fill as they please. Each of these things is a container. They limit how much we keep.

SURFACES

Let's talk about surfaces, and not just flat ones.

For years I had a big, comfy chair in the corner of my bedroom. I loved its bigness and its comfiness, but it was almost always covered in random clothes, so I never actually sat in it. In fact, if I ever desperately needed to sit in that chair (which happened no more than three times in the years it was there), I had to first move all the stuff off it.

That chair wasn't serving the purpose of a chair. I couldn't sit on it. It was a dumping ground and a constant eyesore in a room where I struggle anyway.

I did what always works when I need to stop piling things on a piece of furniture. I got rid of the furniture. I gave away the chair.

Habits schmabits. It wasn't happening. That convenient spot plus my tendency to pile things on convenient spots were too much. I couldn't fight it. Once the chair was gone, the pile was gone.

If a furniture piece has a purpose, that's wonderful, as long as it fits within the container that is my bedroom. But the chair by the side of the bed, no matter its intended purpose, only served the purpose of collecting a mess. Removing the chair removed the mess.

DRAWERS

I told you we were going to tackle closets on their own, because closets are . . . closets (rooms on their own that basically encourage the stashing of stuff). But drawers in dressers that are in the bedroom are part of the bedroom.

First, consolidate. Put socks together, undies together, and T-shirts, shorts, and sweaters together. If you have drawers to designate to each category of clothing, do that.

Drawers are containers. They are natural limits to how much you can have of whatever is in them. You can have as many socks as your sock drawer will hold. You can have as many pairs of workout shorts as your workout-shorts drawer will hold. And if you only have one drawer for all of your workout clothes, then you can only have as many workout clothes (leggings, shorts, and tops combined) as your workout-clothes drawer can hold.

As you consolidate and make things fit, accept your reality. If you have more workout clothes than will fit in your drawer, ask yourself if you buy workout clothes more often than you wear them. If so, they don't deserve drawer space more than the clothes you do wear. Or maybe you live in athleisure wear and can ditch the clothes you avoid because they don't stretch.

If you need to put something in a drawer that's already full, use the One-In-One-Out Rule. Take out a less drawer-worthy pair of socks to make room for the more drawer-worthy pair.

Consolidating reveals *Duh*s. As you're consolidating, match the socks. If there are odd ones, throw them away. As you put T-shirts together, purge the ones you kept only for when you are completely desperate. Get rid of the shorts you never wear because they give you a wedgie.

Basically, be realistic about whether you have passed up the clothes in your drawers again and again. If you'd do the Sniff Test on something from the floor instead of wearing the top that's in the drawer, it's a *Duh*.

KEEPING IT UP

Please know I am still struggling with keeping my master bedroom under control consistently, and though it has improved dramatically over the past few years, I will likely always struggle with it.

The more often I go through these steps, the faster I get this room under control each time. I still work through the steps every time I work in there, even when I'm just "cleaning up" and not officially decluttering, simply because I need focus. The more often I go through these steps, the more often I look around after step 3 and raise my eyebrows in surprise because I'm done. *Done*. After step 3, y'all.

One day as I was diving back into this project, lamenting that it was the bane of my existence to have a magically self-recluttering bedroom, in the middle of my inner tirade I realized I was done. The room looked fine. I realized that sometimes what I think of as an entire Decluttering Project (with a capital D and capital P) is actually just cleaning my room. Just picking up.

It will happen. Eventually. If you keep at it.

Once I realized this, I was more easily motivated to just "pick up" in there. And once I was willing to just pick up in there, I did it more often. And the more often I did it, the more often it was clean and door-leave-openable.

CLOSETS AND CLOTHES

I n this chapter I talk about clothes and the closets that hold them. I'll cover storage closets ("storage spaces") in another certainly wordy chapter coming soon. If you use your closet for both clothing and general storage, look at chapter 17 to help you work through the storage items. I'm going to focus almost exclusively on clothing in this chapter to prevent confusion. Just know that if your attempts to store nonclothing things in this space are making your clothes spill out of the closet, that's a problem.

We'll follow the steps to work through an overwhelming mess, though there are some variations when it comes to clothing.

STEP 1: TRASH

Clothing as trash? Maybe. Not that we're necessarily going to throw clothing in the trash (though we might). I'm talking about stuff that obviously can't be worn.

Ripped things. Stained things. Faded-beyond-usability things.

If you are confident you have nothing unwearable in your closet, yay for you. *Look anyway.* I have a unique ability to think an item of clothing is perfectly fine (because I love it or I love the memories of it), only to one day have the truth slap me in the face.

I'm looking at a photo of it or I'm folding it while a friend is sitting in my living room, and suddenly that top reveals itself as the out-of-style, unflattering garment that it is.

For real. It's embarrassing.

When I was writing this book and more than a little stressed out, I decided to try something I'd always wanted to do that I was positive would make my life easier.

I decided to take our family's dirty clothes to a local laundromat that offers wash and fold service. I was so excited to have someone wash *and fold* our laundry!

I loaded up two large laundry baskets with our clothes from the week before. As I lugged the second basket onto the scale (they charge by weight), I saw a frayed T-shirt collar sticking up from the pile.

I recognized the T-shirt as one my son wears often, but didn't think much of it until the washer/folder filled out my ticket. She added the weight of the two large baskets together, multiplied by the price per pound, and calculated tax.

I would be paying fifty dollars to have someone wash and fold my laundry.

Immediate decision #1: I'm going to keep doing my own laundry like I've been doing for the past almost-thirty years. I am way too cheap to pay fifty bucks for someone to do what I can totally do but just didn't want to do this week.

Immediate decision #2: That tattered-collar T-shirt needs to go. I may be too embarrassed to yank it out of the basket and ask her to reweigh, but I am definitely never again paying good money to have it washed, or even good money for the soap and water required to wash it in my own home, thank you very much.

In that moment, my eyes were opened to the reality of that T-shirt.

I had a reason to see my clothing differently, and I saw that the T-shirt was trash.

You have a reason to see your clothing differently. The reason? You're decluttering.

Go look. If you don't find a single item of trash clothing, great. But most likely, you will. While you're in there, holding a trash bag anyway, remove nonclothing trash.

STEP 2: EASY STUFF

Easy stuff might be coats someone hung in this closet even though you have an established coat closet elsewhere. It might be Halloween costumes that have a designated tub up in the attic but that you never put away last year.

The only thing that has to be done with this easy stuff is to take it where it goes. No decisions, analysis, or even questions needed.

STEP 3: *DUH* CLUTTER

Look for *Duh*s. *Duh*s are clothes that aren't unwearable but that you know for a fact you'll never wear. WDIBTs (Why Did I Buy Thats) and SWDMMTIWWTs (Seriously, Why Does My Mother Think I Would Wear Thats). No angst, no questions, just *Duh*s.

STEP 4: ASK THE DECLUTTERING QUESTIONS

The two decluttering questions don't work as well for clothing as they do for other things. You look for clothing in the closet, and we've already removed the easy stuff that goes somewhere other than the closet. If question #1 helps, use it as you hang clean clothes or fold them to put on shelves.

For question #2, do a scan of the closet, trying to be realistic about whether you'd ever go looking for that blue sweater or those purple boots. If that helps, great. If it doesn't, move on, because focusing on the Container Concept is the best way I've found to declutter clothing.

TWO REASONS WHY DECLUTTERING CLOTHING CAN BE DIFFICULT

First, you must accept that clothing can be clutter. I honestly had no idea. My thinking (if I stopped to think about it) went like this: *Clothing is useful. I have to have it. Socially, there's no way around it. Useful stuff can't be clutter.*

But as I decluttered, found my Clutter Threshold, and experienced how much easier life was with less stuff, I started seeing all the things in my home differently.

I accepted that useful things can *most definitely* be clutter. Anything that consistently gets out of control is clutter, and clothing was consistently out of control in my home. Clothing was clutter.

But another reason I found it so hard to declutter clothing was I never felt like I had enough. Even though floors and chairs were covered in clothing and my laundry piles were almost as tall as me, I felt like I needed more clothing.

I call this the Vicious Cycle of Excess.

The Vicious Cycle of Excess occurs specifically with things that need consistent maintenance or cleaning. Things like clothing and dishes. I wear clothes every single day. Wearing clothes makes them dirty. Dirty clothes need to be washed. When I had no consistent laundry routine, I consistently ran out of clean clothes.

Running out of clean clothes made me do panic-stricken, frantic emergency loads of laundry. That panicked, frantic feeling caused me to assume I needed more clothes, even though there were piles of dirty clothes waiting to be washed.

I bought more clothes so I wouldn't run out as quickly, hoping to avoid feeling that panicky feeling as often.

But then, because I could go longer before I had to wash clothes, I did go longer. The piles of dirty clothes were larger (because they now included the additional clothes I'd purchased) and were even more overwhelming. I put off doing laundry even longer, waiting until I had to do emergency loads and feeling like I didn't have enough.

So I bought more.

Creating a laundry routine helped me gain a realistic understanding of how many clothes we had and showed me which clothes were clutter.

I am not going to give the details of my laundry routine, mostly because I did that in my last book. But I am going to tell you how finding a laundry routine that worked (consistently and long term) in my home completely changed my understanding of clothing as clutter.

I'd always known clothing needed to be decluttered regularly due to growing children, changes in taste, and so on. But I didn't know that even stuff that fit my body or my kids' bodies and was nonhideous might need to go.

When I started consistently washing, drying, folding, and putting away all the clothes in my house on a weekly Laundry Day, Clutter Clothes were ridiculously obvious.

Clue #1: Once all our clothes were clean, it was not physically possible to put them all away in the drawers and closets.

Clue #2: Once all our clothes were clean consistently, we chose to wear certain things again and again and again.

By now I'm guessing the Container Concept came to your mind

when I mentioned clue #1. You're smarter than I was, because I didn't understand right away.

We wore the same clothes every week. When they were all clean on Monday evening, we each chose our favorite shirts to wear on Tuesday morning.

And our favorite undies.

And our favorite yoga pants. (Fine. The yoga-pants thing was just me.)

We had favorites, and identifying our favorites made decluttering simple because we could easily identify which things weren't our favorites. We saw the dividing line between the things we liked wearing and the things we only wore if we had nothing else to wear.

If you are acting on each thing in the book as you read it, go move the donations from the last chapter into the dryer, and fill your washing machine with a load from the pile of dirty clothes.

Because even though clue #2 makes deciding which clothes to keep easier, there's still clue #1 to deal with, and we'll deal with it by using the Container Concept.

STEP 5: MAKE IT FIT

The closet itself is your container. The sizes of existing shelves and rods determine how much clothing you can keep.

Decluttering does not involve finding a way to install new rods so you can justify keeping more clothes. Decluttering is getting rid of enough so the clothing that's left fits easily on the rods you have.

So even though you have clothes in the washing machine, go ahead and declutter to the point that the clothes you have fit into your closet.

Eliminate some things by asking, *What do I hate?*

You know (because I've told you) that I avoid letting emotions into my decluttering process. I do much better when I stick to facts like the physical size of the closet space I have available. But I am okay using darker emotions to declutter clothing. Clothing is strangely emotional in nature.

The *Duh*s are already gone, so I ask a pickier question: *What has one characteristic I hate?*

I may love *one* thing about a jacket. It's my absolute favorite color. I walked straight to that jacket the moment I entered the store (or the garage sale). I was thrilled at the price, and I love the fabric.

But.

But the sleeves are too tight. They dig into my armpits and make me feel claustrophobic. Hating the sleeves means I hate the jacket. If I hate the jacket, I need to donate the jacket.

Step 5.1: Consolidate

Don't pull everything out of your closet. There should (hopefully) be some wiggle room after you purged the trash and stuck the stuff you hate in the Donate Box.

Put all your black slacks together. Put your black dresses together. Put sleeveless colorful tops together. This isn't an exact science, so just go on instinct, and the process will take shape as you go.

If you have fifteen black dresses (I'm not judging, because I totally understand), within that group put the sleeveless ones together, the long-sleeved ones together, and the ones with some sort of pattern together.

Now that all of your black dresses are together, has your perspective changed? Do some of the fifteen reveal themselves as trash or *Duh*s? Maybe the cotton one is obviously faded when you see it next to the others. Maybe now you remember trying on the one with the flouncy skirt every time you want to wear a black dress, but taking it off and wearing the one with the straight skirt instead. *Every time.*

So go through again and pull out *Duh*s that are obvious now that you've consolidated, then remove less favorite things until the clothes that are left fit comfortably in this space. But know this: you don't have to get rid of a single black dress. Your closet is your container, and if you passionately love all fifteen black dresses, keep them.

If black dresses take up your entire closet, that's fine. You just need to be ready to wear nothing but black dresses for the rest of your life. Because if they take up the entire closet, everything else will need to go.

This is your house, and what you keep in your closet is your decision. It's okay. I keep things that make people think I'm crazy too.

For my daughter's eleventh birthday, she invited a bunch of friends over for a slumber party. Besides the fact that they were unbelievably loud all night long, they were truly a joy.

As moms arrived the next morning for pickup, the girls were parading through my living room wearing real formal dresses. They were thrilled to choose from ball gowns and off-the-shoulder satin formals and gold lamé bubble-skirted dresses. They were wearing my complete collection of high school formals.

One mother could *not* believe I still had my high school formals. I just smiled and laughed, but I'll analyze a little for the purpose of this book. We all know it wasn't because I've been perfectly organized for the past twenty-five years.

The container decides how much you can keep. You decide *what* you keep.

I still have them because they fit in my container.

As I cleared my own closet, my daughter was quickly growing out of her princess dresses. When we got rid of her costume stash, my old formals moved into her closet. Her closet had plenty of room, since she's morally opposed to wearing hanger-worthy clothes. (Other than formals, but whatever.)

I'm not going to tell you to get rid of any one specific thing unless it's causing danger to you or your family. But you also don't get to keep *everything*.

You can keep whatever you want to keep, *as long as it fits in your container.* If you want to keep every formal dress you've ever owned, but that leaves no room for any of your current wardrobe, you'd better be fine with wearing lace-covered taffeta to work tomorrow.

The container decides how much you can keep. You decide *what* you keep.

Viewing my closet as a container was incredibly freeing. I didn't have to decide if I loved something enough to keep it. I just had to determine if it fit in the container.

Step 5.2: Purge Down to the Limits of the Container

But what about when the laundry is done?

Don't panic. Some clothes will reveal themselves as Container Unworthy as you pull them out of the dryer. You'll remember throwing them on the floor because they were too small, too itchy, or too wonky. Keep a Donate Box by the dryer so you can stick them immediately in there.

As you put clean clothes away, place them with their consolidated group. If there's no room in the closet, decide if you're willing to get rid of something else to make room (the One-In-One-Out Rule).

If you've worn it recently, you'll likely decide it deserves hanging space. So the question is, what deserves hanging space less? Nothing personal, black pants, you're perfectly fine. But if I have to choose between you and the pair in my hand, I choose these.

HOW TO GET RID OF THE CLOTHES YOU WANT TO GET RID OF

Wearable things that you won't wear should be donated.

But what do you do with nonwearable things? Note: decisions like this cause people like me to hyperventilate.

Different people have *very* different opinions on this subject. Allow me to share the perspectives of the different camps.

One camp genuinely cares about people and hates to throw something away that someone somewhere would be grateful to have. What if a child hasn't had a change of clothing in weeks and would be grateful for this shirt with a hole under the arm? But I just threw it away, and now that child can't perform on her standardized test because she's so self-conscious about her dirty shirt with a big hole that *isn't* hidden under her armpit.

And then the other camp, which also has good hearts, throws anything with the smallest blemish in the trash because they believe it's morally wrong to give something to the poor that you wouldn't wear yourself.

I'm fine with either of these perspectives as long as it means getting clothing you don't need out of your home.

But then there are the people who send me e-mails, completely stressed out because they have read scathing articles on the Internet written by people in both camps. They are paralyzed because they simply don't know which way is best. Their homes stay cluttered with clothes they know they don't want, because they can't get rid of those clothes for fear they're doing it wrong.

And *that* is the only thing that truly is not an option at all: *to keep stuff you know you don't want because you're so stressed out over the best way to get rid of it.*

If you're currently paralyzed, pick one and go with it. And know that the goal is to get to a point where you never again need to do a huge, bag-loads-full purge. Once you're living within the limits of your closet, you won't have to be this stressed anymore.

Here are two valid options for getting rid of imperfect clothing:

Cut them up into rags, and use the rags to clean gross messes. Throw the rags away without guilt, because now they're gross.

That's a valid option, and I've done it. But the Container Concept still applies. I keep rags in my laundry room in a container. That container is the limit to how many rags I can keep. Once that container is full, rag-worthy clothing needs to go in the trash.

Or . . .

(Please read this next section carefully. If you feel the backs of your upper thighs tightening in righteous indignation, keep reading to the end. Okay?)

You can donate these imperfect items of clothing—*if* the place where you donate clothing wants stained and torn clothing.

I used to get angsty and analytical about such things. Then I sat in a presentation by a woman who runs a local charity with a thrift store in my town. Her presentation was about the work they do, but she made a point to ask that we pretty please go ahead and donate stained or torn clothing to their thrift store.

Yes. Really.

They sell these unwearable clothes to a rag maker by the pound, and every cent they get from every ounce of imperfect clothing goes to their cause. She *begged* us not to throw imperfect clothing away.

And then another reseller in my town gave me the exact same spiel when he was picking up donations from my home. *He* brought it up. He asked me not to throw away unwearable clothes, but to give them to him instead. Really.

So it may be worth your time to ask your local donation place. But let me be clear: The goal is to get stuff out of your house. If a five-minute phone call to your favorite donation place will help you get stuff out of your house quickly, make the call. But if the dread of communicating over the phone with people you don't know or the paranoia of doing the wrong thing keeps you from doing anything at all, I'm giving you permission to throw away unwearable clothing.

Do whatever makes it possible for you to start.

Just know that if your local donation place does want unwearable clothes, they still need to be clean. And dry. Stained is a very different thing than dirty. If you wouldn't wear it in this state of cleanliness, wash it before you donate. (Or throw it away.)

Perfection isn't going to happen. You're overwhelmed. But as you change your view of stuff and learn to declutter at the speed of life, you move toward being able to do things more idealistically in the future.

Right now, you just need to get going.

OTHER CLOTHING-RELATED THINGS TO CONSIDER

T-shirt Quilts

Have you seen T-shirt quilts? Quilts made from the T-shirts a student collects during his or her years of school? This is an awesome idea, and I'd love it if someone did that for me. My mother made a quilt out of my childhood dresses, and I treasure it.

But here is a question to consider: Would I *actually* ever do this (either do it myself or pay someone to do it)? *Yeah* . . . that's a no.

If you answered yes, designate a container. Do the research. Learn how many T-shirts are needed for the type and size quilt you want, and then find a container that fits that number of T-shirts. Find the container (the room or shelf) in your home where you will store this container as you collect T-shirts, and start putting quilt-worthy T-shirts in it. Once that container is full, you'll need to use the One-In-One-Out Rule if you get a new one that just *has* to be part of the quilt.

If you've already collected hundreds of T-shirts with the ambiguous idea that one day you might make a T-shirt quilt, choose your favorites up to the number of T-shirts you'll actually need for the quilt.

If you love the idea of a T-shirt quilt, great. Make it happen. But never letting go of a single T-shirt because you have a vague notion that a T-shirt quilt is a cool idea isn't an option. Sorry. If your kid is now a grown adult and you have no plans to make the quilt or hire someone to make the quilt, but can't get rid of the T-shirts, don't skip the Dreams chapter that's coming up.

Use the Laundromat

If the reason you can't move forward on decluttering clothing is the sheer volume of dirty clothes, consider spending an afternoon (or a day) at a Laundromat. If you're that overwhelmed, washing all of your clothes at one time may help you break your paralysis. Just be sure to take a Donate Box (or ten Donate Boxes) with you, so you can declutter the *Duh*s as they come out of the dryers.

Basically, do whatever needs to be done to purge the clothing in your home down to the point where you can manage it. I've covered the most common excuses, but work to identify your uncommon ones and break through your unique hangups to gain control of your closets.

Chapter 16

CRAFT ROOMS AND HOBBY SPACES

Are you wearing steel-toed boots? Because I'm going to step all over your feet.

To be clear, I'm not talking only to crafters. I'm talking to anyone with a hobby: airplane-model-putter-togetherers, paint-by-numbersers, fly-fisherman-thingamabob-makers, knitters, scrapbookers, fishing-reel-repairers, whomever.

And also to be clear, I'm not talking only to people who have designated rooms for such hobbies.

I'm talking to you all. Even those whose unique hobbies I didn't mention, and even those whose craft room is a corner of their living room.

And to be even clearer, I'm not saying you need a craft room, telling you how to turn a closet into a craft room, or even pointing out the horrors of a craft room and telling you to get rid of yours.

I'm talking about whatever situation you have in the house you've got.

Because if there's something I can assume about the people who relate to my clutter struggles, it's that they have hobbies. Lots of them. While I was coming up with that list of examples, I asked my followers on social media for examples of hobbies that require supplies. Oh, wow, did I ever get answers. I got hundreds of answers, and most people shared long lists of various hobbies they loved.

This is a common trait among people who struggle with clutter: they're interesting, and they like interesting stuff.

But before we get to the steps for working through an overwhelming mess in this space, let me ask you an important question: Is your hobby actually your hobby? *Is.* Not was. And not hope-to-be-one-day-so-I'd-like-to-be-prepared.

Is.

We'll dive deep in the chapter about Dreams and Decluttering, but for now I'm just asking the question. I want you to think about this, so as we discuss the realities of this space, you'll already be thinking about whether or not you have the passion to do what needs to be done.

STEP 1: TRASH

Trash is the easiest of the easy stuff.

Grab the black trash bag and start throwing away trash. Paper scraps. Empty packaging. Candy wrappers. Focus first on surfaces, on trash in the visible places. We're following the Visibility Rule to prioritize rooms, but also within the rooms themselves. The goal is to declutter at the speed of life, and who knows when life will happen and this decluttering project will have to be paused?

STEP 2: EASY STUFF

Start looking for easy stuff. What has an established home somewhere other than where it is? Take it there now. Move things to their decision-free homes within the room or in another part of the house. That's easy.

STEP 3: *DUH* CLUTTER

Look for obvious donations: things that make you roll your eyes, shake your head, and wonder aloud why you even have them. Stick those in the Donate Box.

STEP 4: ASK THE DECLUTTERING QUESTIONS

If you start moving something that should be easy and feel a slight hesitation, go ahead and ask yourself the first decluttering question.

Decluttering Question #1: If I Needed This Item, Where Would I Look for It First?

In this room, Decluttering Question #1 is everything, and you need to ask it about any item that's staying in this room. I'm guessing you put a lot of time into this hobby space when you first established it. You had big daydreams about all the time you'd spend in here and all the amazing things you'd create. Maybe this space was, once upon a time, an organizing project.

There's a big difference between where you would look for something first, and where you decided it should go during a big organizing project. If you'd *first* look for colored paper in the accordion file you decoupaged with the wrapping paper from your wedding shower, great. Put the colored paper there.

But if you automatically open the bottom drawer of the desk when you need neon green paper, that is where neon green paper needs to go.

Because that is how the decluttering question works.

You wanted a space for your craft stuff, right? You dreamed it would stay neat and orderly, and make your supplies easy to find, right? "Easy to find" means something's in the first place you look for it.

This was a major mind-set shift for me. I made a conscious decision to organize my spaces for how we live. I stopped putting things in super-logical, well-thought-out places, and instead put them where we look for them. Once I did this, our spaces functioned better and stayed under control longer.

That's another plug for just decluttering instead of organizing.

The second decluttering question will come in handy in this room as well.

Decluttering Question #2: If I Needed This Item, Would It Ever Occur to Me That I Already Had One?

Sometimes (lots of times) hobby rooms become rooms of randomness. Cool stuff gets shoved in the hobby room because there isn't another place for it in the house, or maybe your brain thinks of this as the wouldn't-that-be-cool room instead of the scrapbooking room.

If there's no answer to question #1, ask the second question. And like always, if there was no answer to question #1, the answer to question #2 is probably no, you wouldn't look for it.

Maybe someone gave you everything you need to build designer birdhouses because they know you like to build things. You dumped all the parts in here because birdhouse-building is crafty. But you have no desire to build birdhouses, so you'd never look for birdhouse-building supplies.

Donate them.

Another category of things you'd never look for is maybe-I-*could*-use-this stuff. Stuff you collected for your jewelry-making hobby. You bought it for cheap or accepted it when a friend was decluttering her craft room even though you knew you'd probably never use it.

Question #2 exists to help you realize that even though you love making bracelets, you never go looking for S-hook clasps because you're more of a toggle-clasp kind of bracelet maker.

STEP 5: MAKE IT FIT

It's time to implement the Container Concept. As I'm sure you can predict, the Container Concept is really important in hobby spaces.

Step 5.1: Consolidate

Maybe putting neon green paper in the drawer where you'd look for it made you happy until you realized there were stacks of paper scattered throughout the room. You tried to put them all together, but by the third or fourth deposit, the drawer was full.

That drawer is a container. It's the limit to how much paper can go inside. And possibly, it's the limit to how much paper you can keep.

Limiting paper can be painful. Paper is useful, and you'll probably use all of it eventually.

But if there is more paper than can fit in the drawer, you can't fit it all in the drawer. Pre-deslobification process, I would have immediately started shoving paper into another drawer. Or come up with a fancy new system, *like an accordion file decoupaged with wrapping paper from my wedding gifts.*

But we've already determined the drawer is where you look first for colored paper.

The three choices I thought were my only choices before I understood the Container Concept:

1. Shove. Keep shoving. Smush and push and close the drawer as far as you can. Stop looking in that general direction unless you absolutely have to.

2. Get on the Internet to learn how organized people store colored paper. Spend money on a fancy paper-organizing system, or give up because I didn't have money to spend.

3. Fill another drawer, and then another, and then another

with colored paper. Feel discouraged because I don't have the money for another ten-drawer contraption to store the rest. Or if I do have the money, feel discouraged because this room won't hold another contraption, and I don't have the money to buy a new house.

Now that I understand the Container Concept, I know my favorite paper goes in the drawer first, and any paper that doesn't fit in the drawer goes in the Donate Box. The drawer is the container. It limits how much paper I can keep.

I'm not saying I can't designate another drawer for paper if I really need more paper and there's another drawer available. But if using another drawer would mean displacing scissors and glue and the hole punch, I have to stop and consider the reality of how much colored paper I actually need.

How much colored paper do I use, and how often do I use it? And am I fully aware of how much I have?

If you know you'll use every last piece of the multiple jumbo packs you've found in random places, and you'll use them up *before* you get the urge to grab another jumbo pack, you might need six drawers full of colored paper.

But maybe, just maybe, you don't.

Maybe consolidating the stacks of colored paper pushed your Reality Check Button. Maybe you realized you grab a new package of colored paper every time you go to the craft store. Part of what you're doing in the craft room (or fishing-lure room or sports-equipment-storage corner) is clearing the vagueness. You're eliminating the vague feeling you experience in the paper aisle that makes you grab more paper because you're not sure how much you already have at home.

That's one of the best perks of decluttering: awareness of what you have.

You knew you had colored paper, and you even knew where you'd look for it. That's why you flew through the two decluttering questions.

Step 5.2: Purge Down to the Limits of the Container

"Make It Fit in the Container" is where you're stuck. You had no idea how much colored paper you had, so buying more made sense. You had no idea because colored paper was spread randomly throughout this room or cabinet or space (or your house). It wasn't in its container.

But what about now? How do we solve this very real paper dilemma right this second? In this moment? So we feel like the room is actually decluttered when we're done?

We face reality.

If you consistently go through four packages every single week, you need to keep the paper. Make room for it by clearing other drawers of things you don't use.

If you have a specific project that requires four packages of paper, and it's already on your calendar (not a vague maybe-if-that-ever-happened-I'd-be-ready project), you need to keep the paper. But it may not need a second, third, and fourth drawer, because as soon as you're done decluttering the craft room, you're going to create the file that needs to be printed and start printing. If that's your situation, move the paper that won't fit in the drawer to the printer—now.

But if, just if (and to be clear, this is probably the case for 9.989 out of 10 people who are reading this book right now) you don't already have plans to use four full packages of colored paper over the next two weeks, stick the extra paper in the Donate Box.

Ouch. I'm mean. And hateful. And a flat-out money waster. And I have zero imagination.

Except that we're talking about living comfortably within the house you have, and making this space usable. Usable for crafting. Which involves much more than paper.

There has to be a limit to how much paper you can keep because you need room for other supplies, and you need room to work.

That drawer is the limit, whether or not this is perfectly good paper. If that makes you mad, blame the drawer. If it makes you happy, blame me.

Prioritizing Container Space

There's an entire chapter coming up about decluttering dreams, and in it (spoiler alert), I talk about crafting. And how, as a dreamy, creative type, I think everything creative looks fun. This is a big factor in my clutter issues.

But in this chapter let's focus on the super-practical, essential-for-making-actual-progress stuff.

If your passion for creativity isn't completely focused on one hobby, this room (or shelf or space) may not be big enough to store every last thing you've collected for the general category of "hobbies." You're going to have to prioritize.

Sorry.

We've established that the size of your house is the size of your house. If it's important to you that bedrooms function as bedrooms, the kitchen functions as a kitchen, and the living areas function as living areas, then this space you have available is the limit to the amount of hobby-related paraphernalia you can keep.

Decide which hobbies get priority, starting with the craft/sport/hobby you do most.

Not that you *like* most, but that you *do* most. Not that you *wish* you did most, but that you *actually do* the most. And not even the one you spent the most money on, but the one you actively experience either external or internal motivation to do—and then actually do.

It gets space in the container first. It gets priority.

Even if it's currently spread out all over the surfaces and not put away. If it gets used, it gets a space.

But here's where some people get confused about the Visibility Rule. Following the Visibility Rule doesn't mean you can't clean out a cabinet or a drawer that isn't visible at first sight. It means your goal has to be to make visible progress. If something out in the open deserves a container but doesn't have one, you may need to eliminate something that's been invisible inside a container for years because you never use it.

You've already got a trash bag and a Donate Box ready to go. And for the vast majority of those reading, your feet are attached to your legs and ready to take things where you'd look for them first. If you run across a potato masher in the beads-and-baubles drawer, take it to the kitchen. (It could happen.)

Once you identify leather working as the hobby you do on a regular basis, you know leather-working tools (fasteners, wooden hammers, markers, and so on) deserve container space.

Consider which drawers are full of things for hobbies that deserve container space less than the leather-working tools deserve it.

You may have to acknowledge that your crochet supplies haven't been used in a while. Or ever. Or at least not as often as your leather-working stuff.

Suddenly, the ugly yarn you bought on sale reveals itself as ugly. You knew it was iffy when you bought it, but it was *such* a good deal. But now that you're viewing this space as a container, the iffy/ugly yarn is clearly less container worthy than your leather mallets.

So pull out the iffy/ugly yarn and stick it in the Donate Box. Consolidate things that are left until there's an open drawer for your leather supplies.

Sometimes your eyes will be opened to an entire drawer or shelf full of Not Gonna Happens.

I will never tell anyone that leather working is not a good thing to do, even if leather working requires huge amounts of tools and supplies. Leather working is a perfectly wonderful hobby for anyone who actually works leather.

And that is the key: who *actually* works leather.

Which hobby are you actually doing? That's the one that deserves shelf space.

OTHER RANDOM THOUGHTS ABOUT CRAFT ROOMS AND HOBBY SPACES

When You Only Wish You Had a Hobby Space

What if you have no hobby space but you desperately need one? Maybe you legitimately do your hobby consistently, but you have no place to put the supplies, so they sit in a corner of the dining area or on a card table in the living room. When you need to get the house ready for guests, those supplies and mid-project pieces get shoved somewhere.

Wishing for a house with a craft room doesn't help. But viewing the house you have as a container does. If your hobby is something you do consistently, it deserves space in your home. Find that space by asking yourself what you're storing that doesn't deserve space.

Maybe you're storing a collection of crystal bowls that you got for your wedding. If you have been married almost twenty years and you've never used those bowls, could you donate them and use that cabinet to store the supplies for the hobby you do on a regular basis?

Or are you storing six tubs of baby clothes in the hall closet even though your youngest child outgrew them a decade ago? If you kept only one tub of baby clothes (or none, but I am trying to be nice) with your very favorite baby stuff, could you store your hobby supplies in that closet?

On Maintenance

I know your real question: I can declutter this space, but how do I keep it from going back to Crazytown by next week?

I totally get it. I know how it feels to work so hard on a space and then have it look like a tornado hit it just a few days later.

One of the biggest benefits of just decluttering instead of organizing has been that re-cluttering doesn't happen as easily or as quickly. When I organized, I still had pretty much the same amount of stuff when I finished as I did when I started. When life happened and it got out of control, the same amount of stuff was out of control, and the mess was, again, everywhere.

But when I just declutter, things are *gone* from the space. So when life happens and everything is everywhere, there's still significantly less mess than before. Recovering is simply a matter of putting things away, because I have only things that will fit in the container. Really, this makes life so much simpler.

STORAGE AREAS

Let's talk about the purpose of storage and how your thoughts on storage may have changed significantly since you started this book and this decluttering process.

Has your view of your home changed now that you think of it as a container? Have you enjoyed living with open space and seen the value of the square footage you've added by getting stuff out?

Are you feeling real momentum, having purged so much easy stuff? Are you loving your visible progress? Do you find your decluttering energy is consistently increasing with the more visible progress you make? Has your definition of clutter changed?

Here's the thing: We've gone through the house, room by room. You can apply the skills and steps you've learned to any space in your home, even the ones we didn't specifically discuss, like bathrooms and laundry rooms. But now it is time to talk about storage spaces. They present unique challenges. We're talking about storage spaces last. We followed the Visibility Rule, and storage spaces are usually the least visible spaces.

They're also the hardest spaces to declutter because the fate of *every single item* is in question.

But facing this room now will be nothing like it would have been before you started this process.

The progress you've made will have a huge impact in this space. Things in here will look different to you than they have before.

This isn't going to be like the time you opened the door, pulled a bunch of things out of boxes, felt overwhelmed, and ran out crying.

It's going to be easier. Use your experience and use the steps.

I dread decluttering storage areas. It's my least favorite kind of project.

If you're scared, let me assure you I'm not going to tell you to eliminate all storage areas in your home. I won't even tell you storing things is always bad.

I'll share the perspective changes I've made on storage, but for now, I'm giving you concrete steps for decluttering your storage areas, no matter how chaotic or crazy or overfull they are. Once you've decluttered them (or even as you're decluttering), your perspective on your need for storage will change naturally.

DEFINING THE ROOM

Is this an actual storage space, or is it space you sacrificed so you could store things? Like maybe, a garage.

My garage is my personal biggest storage-space struggle. It's just so convenient for temporarily stuffing stuff. But when I do that, I can't do what I need to do in that space because I'm using it for storage.

Maybe you have a room inside the house that has inadvertently turned into a storage space. I've had rooms like that. I've asked guests to sleep on a sofa bed in the living room because the guest room was piled high with boxes.

Keep your desired definition for this room in mind throughout this project. What do you want this room to be when you're done? A guest room? An office?

Is this box of kid's meal toys from my childhood more important to me than being able to give Grandma her own room? Is it more important to keep the teaching stuff from the job I quit more than a decade ago than to protect my car from the Texas sun? Is this box full of miniature international flags worth giving up a place where I could store my art supplies?

You don't have to answer those questions before you start. Go ahead and start.

STEP 1: TRASH

To get started, focus on the easiest of the easy stuff: trash.

A storage space can be overwhelming. In my home, I assume that behind the closed door, everything is important. A room or closet full of important stuff is totally overwhelming.

Give yourself permission to open the door and look. Take a moment to let your eyes adjust, and look for obvious trash.

Open your mind to the possibility that on one or six occasions, you frantically tossed *something* in there so you wouldn't have to figure out what to do with it.

Throwing away trash is movement, and movement is everything. Once you've done one small thing, you've started, and starting is the key to breaking through Decluttering Paralysis.

STEP 2: EASY STUFF

Identify the easy stuff. Easy stuff has an established home somewhere else, but it isn't in that home.

You may assume nothing in your storage space has an established home somewhere else. If it did, it wouldn't be in your storage space.

Maybe you're right. Maybe you're not. Either way, look for the easy stuff.

Take easy stuff with established homes to those homes.

STEP 3: *DUH* CLUTTER

Any of the steps and strategies may be used at any time in this space, because storage spaces are, by definition, random.

If you pick up a *Duh*, put it in the Donate Box.

*Duh*s will be plentiful in here. This entire room may be a Procrastination Station. You'll likely find things you already decided you didn't need, but for some reason you didn't get rid of them. Maybe you'll find boxes full of things you meant to donate that you collected back before you knew Donate Boxes needed to be donatable. Maybe this is the space where you shoved things you assumed you'd put in a garage sale someday, but you never had a garage sale.

If you can reach something that's easy, stick it in the trash or the Donate Box, or take it where you'd look for it first.

Even if that means shoving something not so easy to the side. Note: "to the side" means still in the space where you're working. I completely understand the temptation to pull everything out of the room, but I will never tell you to do that. You *can* declutter without pulling everything out. Working through the clutter, final decision by final decision, without making a bigger mess is possible. This is how you declutter at the speed of life. Whether you have five minutes to give to this room or an entire week, you'll make progress.

Don't worry (yet) about the possibly-easy-but-who-knows-since-it's-at-the-bottom-of-the-pile stuff.

We're reducing the mess. Less mess means success.

STEP 4: ASK THE DECLUTTERING QUESTIONS

Now that the top layer of easy stuff is gone, look for nonboxed stuff and ask the first decluttering question.

Decluttering Question #1: If I Needed This Item, Where Would I Look for It First?

If you have an answer, take it there. But if your answer is "Uh, in the storage room?" move onto question #2.

Decluttering this room is different than your kitchen. In the kitchen, you wouldn't even pick up a dinner fork to ask question #1 because forks are meant to be in that space.

But in your storage space, every single item requires the questions.

(Aren't you glad we're already done with your visible spaces since you'll be spending a *lot* of time in here?)

Decluttering Question #2: If I Needed This Item, Would It Ever Occur to Me That I Already Had One?

This is *the* big question for a storage space. The first part of the question—"If I needed this item . . ."—will turn some things into immediate *Duh*s.

If not, ask the whole question. If I needed this item, would it ever occur to me that I already had one?

Sticking something into storage lets me tell myself I'm not being wasteful, that I'm thinking of the future. But then when the future comes, I don't remember I have it. Or if I do remember, I often decide it's easier to buy a new one than to dig and shift and search through boxes in my storage space.

No matter what you were thinking when you stored the snow cone maker, if you wouldn't look for it, put it in the Donate Box.

If you feel like your head is going to explode, put the snow cone maker in the Donate Box.

But if your heart is truly breaking, and tears fall at the thought of letting it go, set it aside. Move on to the next thing. Really.

STEP 5: MAKE IT FIT

Now that you're moving, touching things, and asking questions, let's talk more about the goal of this room/space/corner/shelf. Understanding the purpose of this space will have a big impact on this containerizing step.

If things are being stored for a purpose, this space needs to be usable as a storage space. The most important feature of a functional storage space is get-it-out-ability. If there's a reason to store something, it also needs to be accessible.

I know this sounds like a task that's dangerously similar to organizing, which I've promised we're not doing in this book. But the container that is this room needs to also have space for me to walk or reach into it so I can get the things I need when I need them.

The purpose of a storage room is not to hold so much stuff I have to use my full body weight to close the door. (Which is something I've totally done.) The purpose is to keep things I'm going to need so I'll be able to use them when I need them, and this means I have to be able to get to them.

Step 5.1: Consolidate

Put obviously similar things in the same general areas. If you're dealing with a small cabinet, put like things together on one section of the shelf. If you're dealing with an entire room, put like things together in various corners.

Maybe for you, consolidating will play out like this:

What in the world is this Dana woman thinking? There is no possible way to consolidate in this room full of random junk.

(Continued muttering.)

Fine. I'll move this box marked Baby Clothes over here on top of this other box marked Baby Clothes. *(Grunt, mmmph.)* Oh. There are two more boxes of baby clothes.

(Grunt, ugh, oof.)

Huh. A box marked Pots and Pans. I'll put it on top of this other box marked Dishes, because I'm consoli—

Wait.

Pots and pans? Dishes? Really? Um, *why* do I have a box full of pots and pans? I don't even have to ask any decluttering questions. I'd look for pots and pans in the kitchen, but I had absolutely no idea I had *these* pots and pans and would *never* have even looked for them.

I got worked up and tortured enough over pots and pans three weeks ago when I decluttered the kitchen. Everything fits in my kitchen cabinets as they are right now. I purged six skillets and a pasta pot. I know for a *fact* I do not need anything in this box. I can't believe I've been stressed out over not having space to store things and all this time I've had a box—wait, you're kidding—*two* boxes of pots and pans and a box of dishes in here!

(Deep breath.)

Okay. This is easy. I should probably double-check to see if that's really what's in here, and yes. It is. Other than a Christmas stocking I don't even recognize.

Yay for donating an entire box.

Yep, second box is good to go too.

(End scene.)

And now there's more space for consolidating other things.

Like baby clothes. Once I see boxes marked Baby Clothes stacked all the way to the ceiling, I realize maybe I don't need to keep them all. A few baby clothes are cute. Boxes and boxes taking up space we now need for hockey sticks and rollerblades? Not that cute.

But getting rid of baby clothes is not easy for a sentimental mama. I feel the paralysis taking over my soul.

Look. Always look. Remember? I have to make myself look, no matter how sure I am that I know how I'll feel when I open that box.

Because one thing I know for sure after fifteen years of mothering is that I don't have the razor-sharp memory I still seem to think I do. Looking is the only way to know if the stuff inside the box (or at the bottom of the pile) is as emotionally volatile as I'm confident it is.

When I make myself look, I know what I'm dealing with. And usually, I learn I'm wrong. "What? These *aren't* baby clothes my kids wore? They're secondhand cloth diapers a friend gave me that I never actually used?"

"What *are* these toys? I don't remember ever seeing these before in my life. And *this* is the box of old blankets I thought I donated to the animal shelter!"

See how a moment of consolidating can turn into a moment of *Duhs*?

Step 5.2: Purge Down to the Limits of the Container

Again, what is the definition of this space? Is it truly storage space, or is it space you sacrificed in the name of storage?

Storage spaces that aren't defined end up being random spaces. When random things are randomly strewn through a space, it's hard to grasp the reality of how the container is being used. But when like things are together, the realities of the container are glaringly obvious.

Defining the space will help you identify the limits of the container you can use for storage, but even if you have no idea what you'll do with this space once the clutter is gone, keep going.

CONTINUE WORKING THROUGH *ALL* THE STEPS (AGAIN AND AGAIN AND AGAIN)

Once you've made your way through large, out-of-the-box, visible items and eliminated *Duh*s that revealed themselves through consolidating, start working on what seems to be the easiest pile or the easiest box first. Remove the trash, deal with the easy stuff, donate the *Duh*s, ask the two decluttering questions, and consolidate what's left with similar things in the rest of the room.

And remember, it's okay to tackle this room for an hour here or there. Or fifteen minutes whenever you can. Or work without setting any time goal at all, knowing that however much time you spend, you will make progress because you won't be making a bigger mess.

You can do this!

PART 3

Helping Others Declutter

Chapter 18

OTHER PEOPLE'S CLUTTER

There's a pretty high chance you'll be in a position at some point in your life to help other people declutter their stuff. You'll be in that position because you're aware that clutter is a thing, and you've put enough thought into decluttering that you read a book about it that one time.

Which, no matter how organized or unorganized you are, means you probably know and care about decluttering more than the people you're helping care. I don't have a lot of advice on how to make them care, but I do want you to be aware of this fact. Especially if you're helping people who didn't beg you to help them declutter.

People know they have clutter. They want it gone. But they don't know the realities of getting rid of it. And that's what we're talking about in this section. How do you help, using the knowledge you've gained from decluttering your own home? And mostly, how do you do that while keeping the love in your relationship with the person you're helping?

WHAT DO WE MEAN BY HELPING?

There are different kinds of helping. Sometimes you're helping because someone—a friend, an older relative, your child (grown or young)—asked you to help declutter a room, an apartment, or a home.

151

You enter these situations with credibility because the person who asked for your help sees your contribution as valuable. You have permission to discuss the clutter and encourage its elimination.

But your idea of what you'll be doing and the other person's idea of how this will work ~~might~~ will be different. You may be there as muscle or as brains. This person may know exactly what he or she wants done and simply needs someone strong to help do it. Or he or she may feel completely overwhelmed and need your help to make decisions.

Sometimes, though, the person you're helping declutter *hasn't* asked for your help. You'll have to earn your credibility. If you're the owner of the space that needs to be decluttered, you have a say in that space, but if not, your task will be even more difficult. Earn credibility by decluttering your own space first. Make visible progress. Gain momentum. Change your own attachment issues. I promise, people are watching as you do this, and your offers of help will be taken more seriously if the person you want to help believes you have a clue about decluttering.

> **Earn credibility by decluttering your own space first. Make visible progress. Gain momentum. Change your own attachment issues.**

All that was a nice way to say: get rid of your own junk before you tell your husband to get rid of his. Clean up your own house before you tell Aunt Harriet you're coming over to clean up hers.

OVERALL STRATEGIES FOR HELPING OTHERS DECLUTTER

Stick to facts. When a relationship gets strained in the midst of a decluttering project, it's usually because someone feels criticized or there's a power struggle happening. I've eliminated emotions from the decluttering strategies I use in my own home, and this makes them effective strategies to use when helping other people.

Stick to the decluttering questions. As someone who once wanted to keep everything, I did not respond well to someone saying my reasons for keeping something were dumb. Honestly, the more criticized I felt, the more I resisted everything my helper tried to do.

Instead of giving a lecture on the statistical probability of needing to wear a pair of mismatched socks with holes in both heels, ask where the person you're helping would look first for socks. Then let the sock drawer be the bad guy. Stick to the facts by asking which pair of socks to get rid of so there will be room for this pair. Scrunch your face into a sympathetic look and nod when the person you're helping expresses horror at the thought that someone would not keep socks. And then ask again.

Stick to the facts. Acknowledge emotions, but don't engage emotions.

Give people ownership over the process by accepting their instincts. You know by now that an instinct-based answer to Decluttering Question #1 (Where would I look for it first?) is *the* key to making maintainable decluttering progress. This strategy is much more effective than trying to come up with the very best place to put things. When I trust my own instincts, my house functions better and stays under control longer.

When you're helping other people declutter, go with *their* instincts. It's their space, and they're the ones who will be maintaining any progress you make. Your instincts don't matter if you don't live there. You may need to help them trust their own instincts and trust you enough to be honest about their instincts. Every time you ask the first decluttering question, listen to the answer, and then act on the answer, you're both teaching how to eliminate clutter and building trust and credibility that will take you far as you continue to help.

Help others find their Clutter Threshold. You must accept that it will be different from yours.

It might be lower. My mother is absolutely the perfect mother for me, and I appreciate her so much. The only thing I wish she'd have done differently in rearing me was to acknowledge that I had a much lower Clutter Threshold than she does.

Except that I hadn't grown up yet, started a slob blog out of desperation, and made up that term. But whatever.

Find someone else's Clutter Threshold by focusing on less as your goal. A personal Clutter Threshold isn't something you diagnose. It's something you find as you work, and you find it by aiming for less.

Aim for better. I'm a project person, and even though I've learned to combat that unhelpful-for-the-long-term mentality in my own home, when I help someone else, I'm so tempted to think the space has to be perfect before I leave.

It doesn't have to be perfect. As long as the space is *better* when I leave, we've succeeded.

Prioritize people over stuff. I'm not writing this book for professional organizers to implement these strategies with their clients. I'm writing this book for the declutterer. The home declutterer. The average person determined to change her home.

But this section needs to exist, too, since real life is lived with other people.

People matter more than stuff. Don't sacrifice years of love and life lived together over a disagreement about a toaster that won't work. Just don't.

But then there's the flip side. What about when *you* feel undervalued, unvalued, or even demeaned because the person you're trying to help seems to value stuff more than he or she values you?

There's nothing I can do about that. Sorry. I don't even know the person whose clutter popped into your head the minute I said people should matter more than stuff.

I do know, though, how it feels to be in your position. That it's unbelievably frustrating when stuff that has no actual value seems to be more valued than you.

But *you're* reading the book. They're not. Even if you get the audio version and play it on speakers in your home twenty-four hours a day, it's not going to have the same effect on other people that it's (hopefully) having on you.

You were in a certain mental state when you started this book that made you ready to hear what I had to say. You were ready for change, or at least ready to start considering change. This is totally different than if someone walked up to you on the street and started yelling about Clutter Thresholds and drawers as containers.

So, stop. Take a breath, and focus on what you're doing and not doing. And know that as ridiculous as it is to you that this person seems to value stuff more than he or she values you, the idea that you feel so personally offended over this issue seems equally ridiculous to him or her.

Show. Don't tell. Making people sit on the couch while you stand in front of the fireplace and read this chapter aloud isn't the best idea. A lecture on the ins and outs of the One-In-One-Out Rule won't help either.

Asking concrete, logical questions that respect their likes and dislikes does help. So stick to the questions, and respect any answer that actually answers the question, even if it isn't the answer you'd give. Take things where they go as soon as you have an answer to question #1. Look for trash first and put things in the Donate Box immediately if the answer to question #2 is no. Stick to the strategies, and progress will happen.

Don't leave them with a bigger mess. You know by now how to declutter without making a bigger mess, and how to work in a way that allows you to be done whenever life happens and you have to stop. Using these strategies when helping someone else declutter is crucial. If you walk into someone's home, pull everything he or she has kept hidden in a closet onto the floor of the living room, and then have to leave suddenly because the babysitter's dog got sick, you haven't helped, and that person will never accept your help again.

Bow out gracefully. If you can't be kind, don't go in there. Offer to help people find professional help. If you can't control your tongue and you can't avoid getting personal, admit that you're not capable of helping right now, even if you blame it on the headache you know you'll have from the head explosions working on the space would cause.

FRIENDS

Out of all the people in this section, friends should be the easiest. You're friends, after all. If your friend asked you for help, you've been invited to help her make decisions she might be scared to make on her own.

JUST DECLUTTER

I love telling people what to do. I enjoy it so much I often have to physically clench my mouth shut to avoid alienating people in my life. I'm sure they wish I was more successful at this.

Just like I had to focus on decluttering instead of organizing in my own home, I find that when I help someone else declutter, I have to remind myself of this game-changing concept again and again. You may have been invited to help. You may have been begged to help. But today is not the day that you get to fix this person you've always wanted to fix. It's the day to just declutter. Don't get distracted by the shiny idea of changing how she runs her everyday life.

You're there to remove things. You're there to help your friend be realistic as she goes through her clutter. You're there to keep her on track and ask the correct questions.

DIRECT THE PROCESS AND STAY ON TRACK

The main benefit to having a friend help declutter is focus. Clutter is intensely personal, so it's easy to get distracted. You are there to keep your friend on track. Bring her back to the most visible space when the enormity of the overall task threatens to overwhelm her.

Help her identify easy stuff. Hold the trash bag. Move the Donate Box a little to the left. Point to the next thing instead of engaging in the conversation about the sob story that got her into this mess.

Deal with procrasticlutter while your friend works on other easy stuff that needs to go where only she knows it goes. Folding laundry and washing dishes isn't fun, but it's mindless. You can easily ask, "What's easy?" and the two decluttering questions while you work. Dealing with procrasticlutter, no matter how frustrating, is part of the decluttering process. Take that on yourself so your friend can move on to the real decluttering decisions that need to be made.

ESTABLISHING TRUST

You already know the questions to ask. You know the order of the decluttering process that creates visible progress and builds momentum.

When you're helping other people declutter, though, it's incredibly important to listen to their answers. So when you ask, "Is there anything on this countertop that has an established home somewhere else?" accept the answer. If your friend keeps screwdrivers in a drawer in the living room coffee table, don't tell her that's a dumb place to keep screwdrivers. Just smile and take it there. This is how you'll build trust.

Prove through your actions and reactions that you respect your friend and aren't there to completely upheave her way of doing things.

Keep things simple, and stick to the steps without rolling your eyes or asking your friend to defend her answers. Throw away trash, put easy stuff where it goes, and stick *Duh*s in the Donate Box.

After the easy stuff layer is gone, ask, "If you needed this item, where would you look for it first?" Explain that "would" is instinct. When you see the wheels turning in her head, remind her that instinct means there's nothing to analyze.

If you stayed nonjudgmental during the easy stuff phase, you'll have earned the right for your friend to be honest with you during the decluttering question phase. If she seems embarrassed when she tells you where she'd look first, just say, "Okay." Then take it where she'd look for it.

I once heard that for people to be willing to change, they first need to feel accepted as they already are.

As someone who desperately needed to change her ways, I can tell you this is true. I needed to feel accepted by the person who was trying to help me. Feeling judged made me want to defend myself, and this meant defending the way I'd been doing things, even when that way was so clearly disastrous. Asking the two decluttering questions and accepting your friend's answers lets you show that you accept how she does things in her home.

Do, however, try to read your friend's face as she answers question #1. Is she making up an answer? Is she trying to impress you, or does she think there has to be an answer?

If you're not sure, go ahead and ask question #2: "If you needed this item, would it ever occur to you that you already had one?" If she wouldn't look for it, encourage her to put it in the Donate Box.

Consolidating is the perfect job for you as the helpful friend. It's physical work that has to be done, but it doesn't require decisions yet. Put like things together within the space so you can both get a visual reality check. You know by now that consolidating helps teach the realities of the Container Concept without any lecturing whatsoever.

Consolidating is important so you'll be ready to start purging down to the limits of her containers.

If you've dealt with the easy stuff, purged or relocated things by asking the two decluttering questions, and consolidated, there's a 73.456 percent chance your friend is looking a little dazed at this point. But keep going. Be the muscle. Ask her to tell you which things are her favorites, and place those in or on the container/shelf/cabinet/ drawer. As the shelf or box fills up (or if it's already full), point out that it's full, and suggest donating the things that don't fit. If this causes panic, use the One-In-One-Out Rule.

LET MOMENTUM HAPPEN

Momentum is real. If you've followed these methods in your own home, you know this. Don't get caught up in a once-and-for-all mentality when you're helping a friend. Praise the visible progress you're making. Point out the improvement. Celebrate "less" and "better" as you go.

Your friend will get better at answering the decluttering questions, just like you got better at it. She'll start enjoying the diminishing volume of stuff.

EXPLAIN YOUR METHOD

Don't lecture, but if your friend asks, do explain why you're asking what you're asking and why you're working on visible spaces as needed. Maybe let her borrow this book before or after you help her. Feel free to blame this Dana person for your decluttering methods.

HELP YOUR FRIEND FINISH

The finishing is the hardest part of any project, and finishing a decluttering project is the hardest of all. Distractions happen. Exhaustion happens. Fizzle happens.

Be the muscle. Be the walker. Be the one who takes things where they go. Be the one who stays focused on visible spaces so your friend will continue to be inspired by her own visible progress.

HELP MAINTAIN AND RE-DECLUTTER

What's your long-term role as the friend who helps declutter? Let me be clear: it is *not* your job to threaten your friend with an unexpected doorbell.

The only thing that will do is make her start looking for other friends and start phasing you out of her life.

I can say from experience that the least helpful thing for a decluttering helper to do is to be shocked and dismayed at the reappearance of clutter. Shaming me for a space going back to being cluttered doesn't spur me to do better. It spurs me to make new friends. *And not let those new friends inside my house.*

If you really want to be helpful for the long term, offer to help again. Start with the trash again, do the easy stuff again, ask the same questions again.

This time your friend will already trust you, you'll know how her home works, and things will go much faster. And she will see the beauty of re-decluttering and understand how worth her time it is to keep going, no matter what.

KIDS

Decluttering with kids presents unique challenges, but you also have one advantage: they're the kids and you're the grown-up. If they live in your home, you're the one in charge. Guiding and directing is already a natural part of this relationship.

First, let's take a moment to define the rooms you might declutter with kids. Do you have a playroom? Do they keep all toys in their bedrooms? Defining the room is a strategy in and of itself, and it's immensely helpful.

A LITTLE OF MY OWN PLAYROOM STORY

When we were searching for the house where we live now, this is how I described my must-haves to our real estate agent: I wanted three bedrooms, plus all the normal rooms (living room, kitchen, and bathroom), plus two additional rooms.

Those two additional rooms were very important. One would be my eBay room, and one would be a playroom.

Those two rooms were nonnegotiable, but I still considered myself flexible. I was willing to turn a formal dining room, second living area, or fourth bedroom into what I wanted to have. I was willing to be creative, as long as there were definite spaces I could use for those two purposes.

So we looked and we looked and we looked.

Finally, I read an ad in our local newspaper for a for-sale-by-owner home that sounded like it might, just *might* have everything I required.

It did. It wasn't perfect, but there was a second living area and there was an enclosed porch.

I decided the enclosed porch was going to be the playroom. I shopped for elaborate organizing systems. We sorted toys with teeny-tiny parts into various bins. I created a reading corner with fluffy pillows, filled a costume tub with dress-up clothes, and decorated the walls with the kids' artwork.

But soon, because of a lack of consistent pickup times, costumes covered the floor, teeny-tiny parts were strewn across the entire room, and the books were falling off the bookshelves. It was scary, so I avoided going in there.

The longer I avoided going in there, the more horrifying the space became. The more horrific the space became, the less my kids went in there. No one was playing in the playroom because the playroom was a disaster.

It, therefore, was not a playroom. It was a toy-storage room in total disarray.

As I worked on my own deslobification process, I worked in that room. I decluttered. I saw that the less there was in that room, the more my kids played in there.

It's a phenomenon most parents have experienced. Kids are restless with nothing to do as they sit on the floor surrounded by toys. Put those toys away, and the imaginative play begins.

Eventually, I decluttered that room so hard it only had a play kitchen, a baby bed, a little table, and a small bookshelf. Only at that point did it function the way I'd dreamed of a playroom functioning. It was a play *space*.

What's the *real* purpose of a playroom? That's the question. Is it a place for storing toys or is it a place for playing? Because without clear direction one way or the other, chaos happens. When our playroom was a wreck, my kids didn't want to play in it. When they didn't want to play in it, they brought their toys into other parts of the house. Then, when we cleaned up the house, I told them to take their toys to the playroom, but because the playroom was a disaster, that meant literally throwing them on top of the pile.

As we decluttered, we found the kids' Clutter Threshold. The room was easier to maintain, and this meant it stayed play-in-able longer.

My kids were happier with fewer toys. Decision fatigue is a real thing. It may not seem like kids are making decisions, but they are. Playing is a child's work, and having too many choices is paralyzing. Just like I experienced Decluttering Paralysis, my kids experienced Playing Paralysis.

I looked into a room jumbled with piles of random toys and costumes and games, and the sheer chaos made the thought of cleaning overwhelming.

My kids looked into a room jumbled with piles of random toys and costumes and games, and the sheer chaos made the thought of finding *something to play with* overwhelming.

As the playroom stayed under control longer, my kids learned which toys were their favorites. Just like I learned which coffee cup was my favorite when all of them were available to choose from each morning, they learned which toys were favorites when all their toys were consistently accessible.

What if you don't have a playroom? If you don't have one, you don't have one. But we applied all of these strategies to my kids' bedrooms as well. Less is better. Having a playroom isn't a magical solution, so deal with the clutter in the space you do have.

I've made my case for having less kids' stuff, but how does that actually happen? It happens the same way decluttering happens in every other area of the home.

I'm going to talk you through the steps as if you are working together with your child. To be clear, I have no problem with you decluttering while the kids are at school or spending the night with Grandma. (You have to know your child to know what's best for him or her.) But this chapter assumes you're working together.

While working together with your child on his or her room isn't the least bit fun, the long-term benefits make this frustrating process worth your time and effort. Nothing cured me of my desire to collect shoes better than purging huge numbers of shoes. Kids who work through the decluttering process will change their view of stuff too. (Eventually.)

STEP 1: TRASH

Use a black trash bag to prevent second-guessing. Tell your child, "First, we'll do the easiest thing. Let's throw away trash." Throw away gum wrappers, wadded-up paper, the sixty-seven foil wrappers from last month's Easter candy that was all eaten by this single child. (Maybe that's just at my house.)

This is about obvious trash, but it also helps kids understand that part of cleaning up is throwing stuff away.

STEP 2: EASY STUFF

With kids, I find it helps to give very specific tasks, one at a time. Say, "Pick up all the clothes off the floor, and put them in the dirty clothes hamper."

"Help me make the bed."

If this were a normal room cleaning, "Put the books back on the bookshelves" would be the next instruction, but this is a decluttering session, and putting books on a bookshelf is the perfect time to introduce the Container Concept.

Just say, "Put your favorite books on the shelf first." With my daughter, we designated the top shelf of a two-shelf bookcase as the Love It Shelf, and the bottom shelf as the Like It Shelf.

If kids share a room, each could have his or her own shelf or section of a shelf to fill with favorites.

Choosing your favorite books is fun. It doesn't feel like decluttering. But it's the best kind of sorting, because once the bookshelf is full, we already know the ones left are the least loved books.

And this is where you, as the mama, really learn to love the Container Concept. The size of the shelf decides how many books your child keeps. Mama doesn't. There's no power struggle. Mama is just stating the facts. The shelf is full. The container set that limit, not Mama.

Hear me, though. It's so important to *let your child fill the container*, even though *Go, Dog, Go!* may win out over *Runaway Bunny*.

That's how the Container Concept works, and that's why it works so well with kids. Mama names the container, and the person who reads these books gets to choose which books go in the container. If your mama heart can't let go of *Runaway Bunny*, fit it in one of *your* containers (bookshelves) somewhere else in the house.

Rejoice with your kids over the fun of putting their favorite things in that container, but when it's full, all other books get donated.

The container concept allows you to honor their personal likes and dislikes, and lets them make their own decisions without it being a power struggle.

If the container is full, and they find their favorite book *ever*, no problem. Simply explain the One-In-One-Out Rule. "You can totally keep that one! Just take one off the shelf that you don't like as much!"

The choice is still theirs, and the container is still the bad guy, not Mama. Yay for that.

STEPS 3 AND 4: *DUH* CLUTTER AND ASK THE DECLUTTERING QUESTIONS

Maybe I should mention that when I picture the room you're decluttering, I'm picturing my own kids' rooms all the times we decluttered them before we finally reached their Clutter Thresholds. I see a total, knee-deep mess.

Once clothes are off of the floor and books are on the bookshelf or in the Donate Box, use the two decluttering questions. I'm combining this step with looking for *Duh*s since what you see as *Duh*s might not be so obvious to your kids. Unless something is obviously outgrown (clothing or baby toys), it usually helps kids to go ahead and ask the decluttering questions.

Ask Decluttering Question #1: "If you needed this, where would you look for it first?" When they answer, have them take it there now. If they can't answer, ask the second question: "If you needed this, would you remember you already had it?" If they wouldn't, put it in the Donate Box.

I know. You're positive they'll never put a single thing in the Donate Box. But these questions are super simple, and they work better than I expected they would on my own kids. I'm told by others that they work on their kids too. If your child can't answer question #2, make him or her answer #1. And don't worry, the Container Concept will get applied *everywhere*, so that will save the day in the end if she claims she'd look for every last thing in the toy box.

STEP 5: MAKE IT FIT

Consolidate first. You've gone through the room and purged, purged, purged. Supposedly, everything that is left is super important to your child. Now is the time to make the most of the existing containers. Your child already understands the Container Concept because you used it on the bookshelf.

If the tub in the corner was the answer to "Where would you look for this first?" for fifty thousand different items, there's a chance it is overflowing and covering the floor all around it.

Dump the tub into an empty Donate Box. (I know this goes against my normal advice.) Tell your child to put his or her favorite things in the container first, and explain that once the tub is full, everything else will be donated.

Y'all, this works. It works like magic. Anything that doesn't make it into the container stays in the Donate Box. Practice the One-In-One-Out Rule if your child later finds something he or she can't bear to donate.

Continue this throughout the room. You've likely collected many containers over the years in your attempts to get this room under control. Use them, but also acknowledge that the room itself is a container, and you may have too many containers to fit in the room.

> Putting things back needs to be as uncomplicated as possible. Simple storage solutions are better than complicated ones.

As you purge containers, consider: What kinds of containers work and which ones don't? How many containers can the room easily hold, and how much can fit easily in each one?

Easily is the key word here. Getting stuff out is fun. Putting things back isn't. Putting things back needs to be as uncomplicated as possible. Simple storage solutions are better than complicated ones.

My favorite containers are just the right size for one single kind of item. My daughter had thirty-ish Barbies, and they fit in a medium plastic paint bucket someone gave her that had her name on it. Another small bucket contained Barbie shoes and accessories.

We also have a rustic china cabinet in her room. It's basically a tall shelving unit, with open shelves on top and shelves with doors on the bottom. We use those bottom shelves as the limit to how many small containers of art supplies and such she can keep, and the three open shelves on top contain her stuffed animal collection.

Stuffed animals are emotionally laden possessions that are mostly for show in our house. We needed an arbitrary limit to contain them. Since she didn't actively play with them, but couldn't bear to let them go, I let her fill those shelves with her favorites first. I was surprised at how easily she identified the ones she didn't actually care about. And best of all, they're contained (so I'm happy), displayed (so she's happy), and easy to put back when they do get pulled down because they have an established home.

WHAT DOESN'T WORK

There is one kind of container that doesn't work for us: anything that could be called a *pit*.

Like the toy box I was sure was an excellent purchase. Once upon a time, I believed that toy box was going to solve all my problems. I'd seen ones like it go for hundreds of dollars in eBay auctions. Seeing all those people bidding made me sure this toy box was the key to getting my child's room under control.

When I found one at a garage sale for a measly fifteen dollars, I grabbed that thing and dragged it home. I was going to solve all my own problems and then sell that toy box for a profit when my kids outgrew it.

Jackpot, for sure.

I brought it home, scrubbed off the crayon marks, and hauled it into my daughter's room. Within fifteen minutes, we filled it to overflowing. Strangely, though, her room *wasn't* instantly organized. Whatever. Surely this thing would start working eventually.

I was wrong. On the sixth or seventh completely exasperating decluttering session, I realized we *never* used that toy box for anything other than fast and furious shoving sessions. Eventually, I had to admit that the toy box did nothing to keep the room clean.

It was full of random things. Single building blocks, doll clothing, puzzle pieces, broken stuff, and more.

The toy box was a dumping ground. If my daughter wanted to get something out of it, she had to dig, which meant pulling out most of what was in there to find the thing she wanted.

The best thing I ever did was dump the dumping ground. I removed the entire toy box from our home, and once I did, the room was better off.

What I learned from this experience: Nonspecific toy storage is completely meaningless in our home. Having less stuff is the only thing that makes a lasting impact.

We didn't relocate the things that were in that toy box. We decluttered them.

As we continued to declutter my kids' rooms, we focused on things they actually played with, not things I thought they would play with when I bought them. We kept the things they immediately went to when the floor was clear and there was room to play.

Focus on less, be excited about better, and remember that re-decluttering is always easier than decluttering was. Purging today will be exhausting and difficult. But the next time you try, so many of the things that caused drama for your kids this time will be emotion-free. Keep going. I promise it's worth the effort.

ROTATING TOYS

I'm often asked my opinion on rotating toys. I tried it when my kids were small. It worked fine sometimes, and then other times we all forgot about the toys in a box in the closet until they had outgrown them. If you can do it, do it. And honestly, if you forget they exist and eventually declutter the entire box that never made it into rotation? That's okay too!

STORING STUFFED ANIMALS

This is the number one problem parents stress over. The key is to establish a container. We tried making the size of the bed the container, but we don't do well with removing the stuffed animals every night and putting them back every day, so that didn't work well for us.

I mentioned the high shelves we use for my daughter's stuffed animals. This worked perfectly.

You could install some shelves on one wall. You could put up a stuffed animal hammock or build a stuffed animal zoo. You can find places to buy those or instructions to make them online. Or you can even use an unstuffed beanbag chair cover as the container. (Don't try to take the stuffing out of one—you'll regret that.) There are even some specially made for this purpose that have a mesh window so you can see the stuffed animals inside.

Whatever you use, though, you must treat as a container. Have your child fill it with his or her favorite stuffed animals first, and then donate the ones that don't fit in the container. If he or she gets a new one or finds a favorite that missed the initial container-filling, use the One-In-One-Out Rule. Even if you don't believe this will work for your child, try it. I think you'll be amazed.

Chapter 21

OLDER FAMILY MEMBERS

H ere's an unfun subject: helping your older relatives declutter.

I remind you I didn't get into this Decluttering Expert business because I just *love* decluttering. I'm in this strange position of writing a book about decluttering because I desperately needed an intervention, but no one was begging to come in and do the work for me, so I had to do it myself.

I pushed through and dug out of my own cluttered mess, and I learned a lot along the way.

There may be people who get excited to declutter their relatives' homes, but I am not one of those people. I actually don't like it at all. But as with most things in life, it has to be done whether I like it or not.

My husband's parents were in their eighties. We were in the stage where we knew that at any moment, we might have to help them move into an assisted living facility and then deal with almost fifty years' worth of stuff in the house where they lived.

To be clear, their home was always under control, they lived well below their Clutter Threshold, guests could appear at any moment, and there was absolutely nothing for them to be embarrassed about. But forty-eight years in one home meant there was stuff. Lots of it.

Before I share how I helped them declutter, let me clarify some things.

I am the daughter-in-law. Even though we're close and get along fabulously, I'm not their child. I see that small amount of distance as an advantage. I had no personal attachment to the things in my mother-in-law's home other than smiling at the thought of my husband wearing that plaid polyester suit back in the 1970s.

I also don't suffer from Powdered Butt Syndrome in this relationship. Dave Ramsey refers to this syndrome often when callers to his radio show ask how to advise their own parents about finances. Basically, he means that no one likes taking advice from someone whose butt they once powdered. It's reality.

> Do your best to not let *stuff* get in the way of your relationship with this person.

The main thing I want to emphasize, though, is that relationships matter more than stuff. Do your best to not let *stuff* get in the way of your relationship with this person. Some of you will read my thoughts in this chapter and decide you could never be so firm with your loved ones. Some of you will think I'm a total wimp and should get tougher. Your relationships are unique, and you need to adjust for your situation. But always remember that one day they'll be gone, and you'll wish you still had them there to disagree with over the value of a teapot.

Don't get personal. Focus on my nonemotional steps to working through an overwhelming mess. If you feel your emotions heating up, go back to the steps. Be the one to let things go. Redirect as needed. This isn't an opportunity to finally say how much it hurt when your brother got a nicer sixteenth birthday gift than you did. It's also not the time to rehash the same stories you've been rehashing for years. It's time to declutter. You're the helper, so you need to keep the focus.

Present yourself as the muscle. I offer to be the decluttering tool, doing the work while the ultimate decisions are left to the people I'm helping.

This worked well for us as we tried to declutter fairly consistently in my in-laws' home. I would ask my mother-in-law if she'd like to clean out anything. If she said she didn't need any help, I suggested something: "Would you like to clean out your linen closet? A kitchen cabinet?"

I knew she didn't get to these things because she couldn't bend over, sit on her knees, or reach the very back of a cabinet. I *can* do these things, so I kept bringing it up until she let me.

I came to the space we were working on with my supplies in hand. I had a Donate Box and a black trash bag. My mother-in-law sat on the seat of her walker, and I pulled things out of the linen closet.

STEP 1: TRASH

If there was obvious trash, I stuck it straight into the trash bag without asking, though I didn't try to hide anything.

I did ask if she saw any trash that I could go ahead and throw away. If something "wasn't trash," I accepted that declaration and moved on to the next thing. This wasn't my stuff; it was hers. (Even though I knew I'd have to deal with it later if I didn't deal with it now.)

STEP 2: EASY STUFF

I asked, "Do you see anything that's supposed to go somewhere else?" And then I took it there. Usually while I was taking the item where it went, she identified more easy stuff.

STEP 3: *DUH* CLUTTER

I asked, "Is there anything in here you already know you want to donate?" If there was, I stuck it in the Donate Box.

The same thing happened in this situation that happens when I work on my own spaces. The overall volume of stuff diminished. As it diminished, it was less overwhelming, and we both found it easier to identify trash, easy stuff, and *Duh*s.

STEP 4: ASK THE DECLUTTERING QUESTIONS

The two decluttering questions work when I ask myself, but they are also great when I'm helping someone else declutter. Their lack of emphasis on emotions is especially helpful in a relationship full of emotions. They reveal whether there's a place for something in the house and if it's something they actually need or use.

Do you know what questions aren't the least bit helpful (like, at all)? "Why do you have this?" or "What were you thinking when you stuck this in here?"

I'm speaking from experience here. When people asked me *those* questions, I immediately became frustrated. I felt defensive and suddenly wanted to hold on to everything. All of it. Because once I felt defensive, we were in a war for my stuff.

Do not put the person you're helping in a position of defending why he or she has something.

Stick to the task of decluttering.

So many times, in family matters especially, simple things turn into power struggles. Sticking to the two decluttering questions (and only two) helps keep things on track.

Decluttering Question #1: If I Needed This Item, Where Would I Look for It First?

Ask, "If you needed this _____ (hairbrush, spatula, bottle of paint), where would you look for it first?"

If the person you're helping starts imagining a scenario, just re-ask the question: "But where would you look first?" Just like you got better at answering that question, he or she will get better as you keep going.

And the best way to help people answer the question truthfully is to prove you're really asking where they'd look first. This isn't a test, and you're not judging the answer. Prove this by taking the item in question where they'd look first, immediately.

As someone who once had well-meaning friends and relatives try to help her, I believe this is the point at which the process broke down. First, we weren't asking the right, nonemotional question (because I hadn't invented it yet). But second, even if we did stumble on the right idea, we'd discuss the answer. And discussing the answer to "Where would I look for it first?" is basically asking, "Where *should* I look for it first?" And when the key word was *should* instead of *would*, the helper's opinion mattered. But the helper wasn't there in my daily life, so I ended up with things in places where I'd never actually look for them.

Clutter is embarrassing. Letting someone help you declutter makes you vulnerable. Every time you take something to the place people say they'd look for it first, you're building trust that you're going to listen to them without criticizing.

Asking where *they'd* look first is giving respect to how they do things in their home, even things that don't make sense to you.

A few years ago, before we all had smartphones, we decided to order pizza while at my in-laws' house. I asked my mother-in-law where her phone book was.

She heavy-sighed and said she had no idea. For years she kept it in the bottom of her china cabinet. But someone had cleaned out the china cabinet for her and moved the phone book to a much better spot. Better, except she had no idea where it was.

The same thing happened to me with plastic Easter eggs. One year I couldn't find them. They weren't in the cabinet above my washing machine where I had kept them for years. That year we didn't hunt for eggs, because I never did find them and didn't want to buy more. Months and months later, as I was putting blankets up on the top shelf of my linen closet, I saw them.

I knew immediately that my mother had moved them there, since she's the only person who would have been deep enough in my home to do that. I asked why she put them there, and she said that while she stayed with my kids when my husband and I were out of town, she'd seen them sitting on the floor of the laundry room and decided to find a "good" place for them.

But that wasn't helpful. They became completely useless when I couldn't find them.

Ask where the people you're helping would look for something first, put it there, and they'll find things in the first place they look. That will get you invited back for more decluttering!

Decluttering Question #2: If I Needed This Item, Would It Ever Occur to Me That I Already Had One?

Only ask this question if there's no answer to question #1. If people are adamant they'd know they had it, then ask question #1 again. If they don't know where they'd look for it, suggest that the answer to question #2 is that they wouldn't look for it, and suggest putting it in the Donate Box.

If they can't answer either question and aren't willing to get rid of it, move on. Leave it in this space, and hope the next step will help them let it go.

Remember your goals are "better" and "less," so progress is

everything. Keep moving forward. Stopping to argue about a deck of cards that's missing the ace of spades isn't worth stopping the progress.

STEP 5: MAKE IT FIT

Step 5.1: Consolidate

Put like things together. Fold tablecloths and stack them. Put pillowcases together. You're "being the muscle" anyway, so do the work that requires no decision-making or emotion. Consolidating opens my own eyes to the realities of my own stuff, and I find it helps the people I'm helping as well.

Step 5.2: Purge Down to the Limits of the Container

Again, stick to the facts. If you're sure the tablecloths will be too tall for the shelf when they're all stacked together, ask them to point out their favorite ones to put in first. As the space gets filled, they'll have already identified their favorites and very likely be willing to get rid of the ones that don't fit. If they're not willing, ask what other things (hand towels, washcloths) they'd like to eliminate so there's room for all of the tablecloths.

All decisions are theirs, not yours. And respect their decisions while sticking to the facts about the size of the container.

Let the Container Be the Bad Guy

If we're talking about messes like magazines in stacks on the floor, offer to fill the nearby magazine holder or shelf. Ask them to point out their favorite magazines first so you can place them on the shelf first. Once the shelf is full, mention that the rest will need to go.

I know. They may be horrified.

But you honored their choices and you helped. So keep that

going, play dumb, and say, "Oh, I'm sorry. Well, which do you want to keep? Sure! No problem! Which ones on the shelf do you want to get rid of so there's room? None? Oh, well where are some empty shelves where I can put the rest?"

I know. It may not work. But the space will be better off than it was, because now the favorite magazines are on the shelf. And you'll have introduced the reality of the Container Concept. Maybe next time they'll accept it.

IMPERFECT DECLUTTERING IS BETTER THAN NOT DECLUTTERING

The goal is less. Any decluttering project that ends with less than you had when you started is a success.

When time is limited and people are uncooperative, it's hard to leave without feeling as though your effort was wasted.

But we're decluttering at the speed of life, remember? And life goes on. The first time you help your relatives declutter is a test, and your goal is to pass that test. Be trustworthy. Be helpful. Don't judge. If you leave a space that's more functional and nicer than it was before, they get to live with that space after you leave. Living with that decluttered space will make them ready to declutter the next one, and you'll start the next project so much further ahead than you did this one.

A FEW MORE THOUGHTS

Hoarding

If you're dealing with true hoarding, you will likely need professional help, especially if you are concerned for your relatives' health or safety. If they understand there is a problem, want to change, and have asked for help, go through the steps, no matter how severe the mess, and see if they're really ready to let you help.

Help with Meaning-Tos

If your relatives are resistant to you helping them declutter, offer to help with things they've been meaning to do. If they have a bag of donations, take it to the local charity for them. If they have a box full of papers to shred, take them to an office store to be shredded. If they don't trust that the people at the office store won't steal their personal information, offer to take them with you to watch the papers get shredded.

If they've heard of this thing called *Craigslist* where every little item gets top dollar and they won't donate because they believe their stuff is worth money, offer to help them set up listings and arrange the details for them for their safety.

If the house is just a complete mess, help them catch up on the basics. Do the dishes. Help with laundry. If they have way too much stuff to fit in their kitchen, wash everything and help them attempt to put it away so they can see there is too much. Basic housework is difficult to argue against, so focus on that, and let it show the need to declutter.

Chapter 22

SPOUSES

This chapter is the last one about helping others declutter. It's also the most difficult and will need the most caveats.

Friends could have varying degrees of closeness, history, and trust, but you can follow the steps and advice and make it work. And if it doesn't go well, you can find new friends.

Kids could mean boys or girls, nieces or nephews, stepkids or foster children, or a myriad of other unique variations on adult/child relationships. Each of those variations color your interactions. As the adult, you're in a position to direct the decluttering process, ask the questions, and work together.

Your relationships with senior citizens may get covered in the Friends chapter, or you may be dealing with your own parents or older relatives, which has its own minefield of issues, for sure. But still, you're likely going into their homes with the express purpose of helping them declutter.

But spouses are their own situation.

Going forward I'll say *husbands*, because in general, it's wives who talk to me about their frustrations with their husbands and clutter. That's the angle from which I have experience, so that's the angle from which I'll speak.

Fact: You're partners. This is very different from your relationship with your children. While it's perfectly acceptable for Mom to announce a time to clear out the kids' rooms and ban all fun until it's done, this isn't how a spouse should be treated. I personally don't enjoy being treated like a child, especially when it comes to someone criticizing my clutter issues, and I know this is the generally accepted truth for all adults.

So in this chapter I'm not going to work through the steps to dealing with an overwhelming mess. You know those by now. I'm going to talk about what *you* can do.

Because what you can do is all you can do.

GO AHEAD AND DECLUTTER

Declutter your own stuff. Declutter stuff that's neutral, such as towels or plastic cups. If one of the things I just named is the one thing your spouse refuses to declutter, then choose something else that's neutral.

But go ahead. Make progress. Purge your own wardrobe and the kids' clothing. Consolidate the kitchen utensils, and get rid of the fourth and fifth potato mashers.

You cannot control another person. And in a good marriage, you shouldn't *want* to control the other person. So control what you can control while also respecting that this is your husband's home too.

GIVE HIM A CONTAINER

In my one hundredth podcast episode, I interviewed my husband. One of the questions submitted by listeners for him to answer was "How has Dana helped you declutter?" He mentioned that I gave him a special space to keep his 1980s memorabilia, and that made it easy for him to decide what to keep because he filled it first with his favorite things. I said, "Oh, yeah. The Container Concept."

He said, "What?"

And I laughed. He had no idea I was implementing limits and practicing my biggest game-changing decluttering concept on him. He just knew I was nice enough and respected his love of his memorabilia enough to give him a place to put it.

DO NOT MAKE DECLUTTERING A POWER STRUGGLE

When your spouse doesn't seem to even care what the house looks like, it's difficult. But a power struggle is never healthy in a marriage. Again, do what you can do; control what you can control without trying to get the upper hand. My mother's best marriage advice was to never say "I told you so." While everyone likes to be right, no one likes to be wrong. And no one likes the person who reminds them they were wrong.

The only reason to ever say "I told you so" is to point out that you won the power struggle. Just don't. Be happy for the change, and don't turn him against you once the change has happened.

TRUST THE POWER OF DECLUTTERING MOMENTUM

It worked with my husband, and it has worked with many others. As he experienced how much easier it was to live with less stuff after I decluttered my stuff and neutral stuff, his view of stuff changed, and his grip on the things I thought he'd never give up loosened. But this *only* happened after he watched me be willing to give things up for the sake of an easier-to-manage, more comfortable home.

ACKNOWLEDGE YOUR PROBLEMS MAY BE DEEPER THAN THE CLUTTER

If you can't communicate kindly when it comes to clutter, there's most likely a communication problem that's about more than just clutter. Consider counseling. Or read a book on communication in marriage. Or both. (I'm not a marriage counselor. I just declutter.)

Chapter 23

ACCEPTING HELP

B efore I finish this section on helping others declutter, I need to address another angle of this issue: accepting help.

Some of you are in situations or have health challenges that mean you need help even if you don't want it. Letting someone help is harder than it sounds like it should be. It's even harder when you've been trying to hide your clutter issues from the people in your life.

When my boys were toddlers, a friend suggested that because we had kids who were close to the same age and played together well, we should set up cleaning days. She'd come to my house one week and help me clean. The next week, I would go to her house and help her clean.

It was a fabulous idea.

But I hemmed and hawed and didn't agree. I was too embarrassed. I was so overwhelmed by my messier-than-she-had-any-idea home that I couldn't gather the energy to do the pre-cleaning (decluttering) I'd have to do before I would let her into my home.

More than a decade later, I still regret that I didn't jump on this amazing idea.

When my second son was born, a close friend who lived in my neighborhood wanted to help me out. She offered to clean my house.

Truly, that would have been the most helpful thing, and she identified it and offered it.

I said no.

I wish I had a time machine to go back and shake some sense into New Mama Dana. I was just too embarrassed. Letting someone past doors that are usually closed and locked makes you vulnerable.

But if you read the previous chapters and thought, *I wish someone would come and help* me *like this*, let me be honest about your role as the helpee. The way in which you accept help and treat your helpers will determine how much progress you make and how willing your helper is to keep helping.

You're already doing the most important thing: you're mentally preparing to let things go. You're reading a book about decluttering, trying to be realistic about your own home, and changing your mindset about stuff in general.

So step 1 is to finish this book.

Step 2 is to start throwing away trash as best you can. If you are physically capable, keep throwing away trash until the moment help arrives. Do the easy stuff. Put *Duh*s in Donate Boxes.

Do what you can, whenever you can, as often as you can.

You might work for days, or you might only have the stamina to work for five minutes at a time. Do what you can, whenever you can, as often as you can.

This will do two things: it will help you get past some of the easy stuff, so when your helper arrives, you'll be ready to use his or her muscle and motivation to tackle the not-so-easy stuff.

It will also start to change your perspective. I cannot properly explain this phenomenon. Doing the easy stuff changed my thought processes. My attachments changed. My view of my stuff changed. My confidence in my ability to survive the loss of my treasured possibilities changed.

But that only happened as I got stuff out of my house. Even though you don't believe your love of your stuff could ever change, throw away trash. Maybe you'll be the exception and your attachments will remain strong. But even if they do, you'll have less trash in your home.

PAYING FOR HELP VERSUS ASKING FOR FAVORS

If you need help, you have two options. You can pay someone or you can ask someone you know to help you.

Paid Help

The biggest advantage of paying other people is they are obligated to help you because you're giving them money. There is also some comfort in not having a prior relationship with the person who is coming in to deal with your clutter. Anonymity can be a good thing. You may be motivated to cooperate in a way you might not with family members.

Paid helpers will (hopefully) be objective, not bringing their history with you or their knowledge of your typical excuses into the equation. They don't know the ins and outs of your unique situation, and they will help you see your stuff from the perspective of someone without any personal attachment to it.

I have never paid someone, but going from what I've heard from people who have e-mailed me, I recommend that you hire someone specifically for decluttering rather than organizing. Be honest about your real situation and your real goals. Ask friends for references. Also, check the websites or social media pages of the people you're considering to get a feel for their personalities and methods to see if they'll fit your needs. Ask them to come by to give you an estimate on how much time they'll need to help you, or set up a single initial session to work on a specific area so you can see if you'll work well together. I've heard stories from people who are forever grateful to the person they hired, and stories from people who burst into tears of frustration the moment the person left.

The possible disadvantage of hiring someone is that you're paying good money and don't want to waste it, and this can make the natural frustrations that occur with decluttering even more frustrating.

Since all work will be "on the clock," you won't have time to go into long explanations of why you want to keep certain things. And depending on the level of your clutter, you may find it isn't possible to do as much as you'd like in the amount of time you can afford.

If you read the section about helping others and wished for someone who would be the muscle for you so you could direct the process but not have to do the grunt work, consider hiring someone to come in and do the physical labor of decluttering under your direction. Ask friends if they know someone who would like to make some extra money, and offer to pay by the hour or by the day. A college student home on a break might like the opportunity to earn money this way.

Most of all, know that hiring someone to declutter isn't a magic pill. Your mind-set will need to change along with your home, and no one can change your mind-set but you.

Accepting Volunteer Help

Free help is wonderful, but there are things to consider.

Was this your idea or your helper's idea? If you initiate the discussion, you can name the area where you want to start (the most visible area) when you ask for help. This will give direction to the work you do together.

If helping you declutter is someone else's idea, accept the help and be thankful for it. Just say you want to work in your living areas (your visible space) first.

Honestly, if a family member wants to help you declutter, you're already over the first hurdle: admitting you have clutter. Someone has noticed your clutter and wants to help you. Go ahead and discuss where you'll start, so you can be mentally prepared to work on that area when your helper arrives.

You are at the mercy of your helper's schedule, so be ready to work when he or she is available to help you. Be ready to accept the help when it's available, and be willing to work according to the other person's style of decluttering.

LESS AND BETTER AND FINISHING

If you have someone helping you declutter, you're in a unique situation now that you've read this book. You know specific strategies and the order in which to do them. But there's a decent chance your volunteer helper hasn't read this book, and either uses other strategies or doesn't realize there are such things as "decluttering strategies." Explain that you've read this book and that the strategies in it make sense to you, and you'd love help following them in your home.

But if your helper wants to do things his or her way, let it go. Help is help, and maybe the progress you make will make it easier to use these strategies on your own.

The main strategy you need to insist on following is decluttering without making a bigger mess. This may mean you spend your time taking things where they go immediately as your helper pulls things out. If you're not physically capable of taking things where they go immediately, and your helper isn't willing to do that, know that your job after he or she leaves will be to eliminate Keep Piles and Keep Boxes as quickly as you physically can.

Decluttering isn't easy. It's heart-wrenching, takes time, and requires changing the way you've done things in the past and the way you view your stuff. Having someone help you, whether paid or unpaid, can be stressful. Make a conscious choice to view it as a positive thing, as a blessing that will help you move further in your own decluttering efforts more quickly than you could move alone.

PART 4

Special Circumstances in Decluttering

Chapter 24

FORCED DECLUTTERING: WHEN IT ALL HAS TO GO

Honestly, the only time I can think of when it *all* actually has to go is when you're dead. And at that point, I'm assuming you won't care.

But there are many times when it might as well all have to go.

Like moving. Or cleaning out the home of someone who has died.

In the time since I started my deslobification process, I have not moved. I still live in the house where I hit rock bottom. This has given me the advantage of writing from the perspective of the person who is in the hardest decluttering situation of all: decluttering because it's the right thing to do, not because they're forced to.

But as a "leading Decluttering Expert" I've been asked about forced decluttering way too many times to not address the issue in this book.

So I'll clarify before I start: This chapter is theory. I'm not a fan of sharing decluttering theories. I've built my strategies according to what works in my own real life. Take this as what it is: a plan I've created based on what I've learned about my unique brain quirks and what does and doesn't work in my relationship with stuff. I'm focusing on what I now understand that I totally didn't understand the last several times I moved.

MOVING

A new home is a container.

When I looked at homes before we bought or rented them, I didn't see them crammed full of stuff, either in reality or in my mind's eye. I was drawn to homes with carefully placed objects and open space. I was always disappointed when they looked nothing like that after we moved in. I didn't understand that the people who lived there when I saw the home were living within the limits of a container.

What I Did Wrong When I Moved

I paid no attention to suggestions of how many boxes I'd need. I assumed there was something wrong with the people at the rental truck company when their estimates didn't work in our house.

What I Think I Would Do This Time

I would use a "moving supply calculator" to get an idea of how many boxes I should be filling. I searched those words online and quickly found several options.

But the questions asked in the calculator I used were geared toward "your home." The form asked questions such as, "How many bedrooms do you have?" and, "How many walk-in closets do you have?" It also asked if the amount of stuff we had was less, average, or more than most. When I answered those questions, I automatically thought of the house I'm in now with the stuff I have now. But that's the wrong way to answer.

For years I assumed my *next* house would cure my clutter issues. For years I was wrong. I took my stuff from one overfilled home to another that was immediately overfilled. I recommend filling out the moving supplies calculator info with the information about the house where you're moving. And answer *average* to the question about how much stuff you have.

Buy the number of boxes the calculator recommends. Even if their recommendations are not perfect, my predictions were shockingly far from perfect, and a moving supply company has some experience with moving. They have to know better than I thought I did.

Use the recommended number and size of boxes for the space you're moving into as your reality check, your Container Concept in action. Those boxes are your containers.

Just as you'd fill a kitchen shelf with your favorite plates first and then stick the ones that don't fit in the Donate Box, fill the recommended number of boxes with your favorite, must-have items first. Things that don't fit in the container of the moving boxes get donated instead of moved. Do this room by room.

> For years, I assumed my *next* house would cure my clutter issues. For years, I was wrong.

I filled out the calculator with no information checked other than "kitchen" (as if the house only had a kitchen and no other rooms), and it told me the standard boxes recommended for a kitchen. Use this strategy to divide the boxes properly so you don't end up using every single box for a three-bedroom house just on the kitchen.

If your goal, after reading this book, is to live in your container, this is a concrete way to make that happen. You can always buy more boxes later if needed.

Follow the Steps

If you're overwhelmed with the sheer volume of stuff in your home, and the thought of sifting through the mess in search of the best things to put in your boxes makes you want to call your realtor and tell her the deal is off, take a deep breath.

Start going through the steps for dealing with an overwhelming mess. Grab a trash bag. Go through the living areas first, then the kitchen, and keep going from there.

Throw away trash, and move the easy stuff to its established homes throughout the house so it will be in the right set of boxes when you unpack. Donate the *Duh*s.

You're lucky, because you get a bonus decluttering question: Would I pay to move this?

Even if you're not hiring movers, you're paying with your own muscle and your own sweat. You're paying for a bigger truck than you need, and you're paying with extra gas costs and time if you have to make an extra trip for stuff you don't actually want.

"Would I pay to move this?" is kind of like the Head Explosion Rule. If the question makes you say, "Uhhh," get rid of it.

Procrastination Stops Here (Ideally)

I love deadlines. Love/hate them, at least.

My love of deadlines is one of the reasons I struggle with procrasticlutter. I think to myself (and sometimes out loud), *I'll have to deal with that at some point, so why bother now?*

But I always, *always* regret that thought.

Your moving day is your deadline. You will declutter more as you unpack in your new home, but don't put off making a decision. Answer the two decluttering questions as you pack.

When I taught in Thailand, a parent of one of my students shared her packing comedy/nightmare. The company sending them to Bangkok had paid for movers to pack their stuff. They packed everything. E-v-e-r-y-thing. So as she unpacked, she found a black trash bag full of garbage that had traveled overseas.

Go ahead and declutter now so you don't end up unpacking trash.

Declutter as You Unpack

Even if you declutter your entire home and pack up only the things you need, you'll likely have the opportunity to declutter more when you unpack. Since you have to put things away anyway, use the two decluttering questions to decide where you'll put them.

If you can't answer the questions, mark one of your bazillion moving boxes as a Donate Box, and get rid of it now.

Embrace your new container. As you unpack, you're no longer in Hypothesis Land. The moving supplies calculator gave you an estimate, but now you don't need to estimate. You're no longer dreaming of how this new home will solve all your clutter problems. The only thing that will solve clutter problems is living within your new container.

As you put away hanging clothes, make them fit. Hang your favorites first, and donate the ones that won't fit comfortably on the bar. Put away your favorite coffee cups first, and donate the ones that don't fit in that cabinet.

CLEANING OUT A LOVED ONE'S HOME

I'm going to talk about the overall process, and I'm going to talk about it as if you are the only one who is going through this process— the one person decluttering the deceased family member's home who has the authority to make decisions about everything in it. Doing this with other family members adds a layer of complexity I'm not qualified to address, neither psychologically nor legally.

Maybe you could send them a copy of this book, or play the audio version aloud as you work together. (Sort of kidding. Sort of not.)

If you have all the time in the world available, I recommend decluttering your own home first. Nothing has changed my view of stuff and given me proper perspective on it more than the act of decluttering. Every time I go through a stack of paper, I start giving the stink eye to any new paper that threatens to enter my home.

Every time I purge old towels, I start rolling my eyes at the idea of Grandma's sentimental but not-brand-new-and-extra-fluffy-and-oversized towel entering my home.

The reason to declutter your own home first is to avoid bringing home more than will fit in your own container (your house). If you don't have time to declutter your own home first, take some pictures of it. Grab your phone and walk around your house, getting photos of entire rooms, closets, and even behind cabinet doors and inside drawers. Do this so when you're tempted to bring something home, you will know for sure whether there is space for it in your home.

Once you're inside your loved one's home, work your way through the steps for dealing with an overwhelming mess. Start with a trash bag (or a jumbo box of trash bags). Feel free to go through the entire house with this step first. That will give you a realistic understanding of the decluttering you'll be doing over the next days/weeks/months.

If this step alone (the trash) is completely overwhelming, look into renting a Dumpster.

Consider how you'll get rid of the majority of stuff in the home. Will you host an estate sale? Will you donate all of it?

If you're planning to hire an estate sale company, ask friends in the area of the home for recommendations now, before you get far into the process. Interview some of the ones recommended, and get their perspective on what your role will be in the process. Will they charge you a flat fee and/or a percentage of the proceeds of the sale? How much will they be involved in categorizing and organizing the sale? Who will be responsible for getting rid of the things that don't sell?

If you decide to hire someone for this, your job is now to remove the things you do want to keep before they take over.

If you will do the majority of the work yourself but plan to sell some pieces to an antique dealer, load up your car with as many of those items as you can on the first day (or, at most, the first week), and take them to sell or be appraised. If you are planning to personally list them for sale online, choose three items you are certain will bring a lot of money and list them for sale today. This is your reality check. If you sell them, you'll gain the experience of selling, and you'll be able to keep on selling things as you continue decluttering this home.

If you go to all that trouble and the antique dealer doesn't want anything you brought, or the online listing brings no interest at all, your perspective on the other things in the house will change.

Do not start making a pile or a room of all the things you'll sell one day when you have the time.

I am going to continue with instructions as if you're donating instead of having an estate sale. Either way, start boxing things up.

Emotionally, nothing compares to how hard this job is, but physically it is simpler than moving your own home because the vast majority of stuff in this house will be donated.

But please follow this advice: don't take anything to your house that won't fit in your container.

I know. Saying that is mean and insensitive. But containers have no emotions. They are impersonal limits. They are cold, hard facts. It's not me; it's the container.

If you want to bring something home with you, ask yourself the two decluttering questions before you even carry it to your car. If you have an answer to Decluttering Question #1 (Where would you look for it first?), then grab your phone and look at the photos you took of that room before you left your house.

Is there a place for it? Are you willing to get rid of something else so it will have a space in your container?

The size of your house is the size of your house. The size of your kitchen is the size of your kitchen. You can totally bring home your mother's spaghetti pot. You'll just have to get rid of the spaghetti pot you already have to make room for it.

The Earth felt like it stood still when your mother died. Your life came to a screeching halt. But your kitchen cabinets didn't grow larger. I'm so sorry.

If you can't answer Decluttering Question #1, move to the second question: Would it occur to you that you already had one? Is it something you'll ever use? If you wouldn't use it, but you love it so, then how will you give it a place in your home so you can treasure it properly?

Can you keep *one*? Is there one platter or one serving spoon that will remind you of your mother's holiday dinners? Will her rolling pin remind you of the biscuits she slathered in butter?

Running across one sentimental item brings all the feelings back to me. Tripping over a stack of boxes full of sentimental items brings pain to my toe.

Replace—Don't Add

If you're living in an empty house with no furniture and few dishes, feel free to bring all the stuff from this house you're decluttering home with you. But if you are already living with everything you need (or more than you need), that is simply not an option. If you're at the capacity of your container already, replacing is the only option. If something comes into your home, it needs to replace something else. If you aren't willing to let your mother's slow cooker replace your slow cooker, hers needs to be donated.

Chapter 25

DECLUTTERING DREAMS (SMALL ONES AND BIG ONES)

At one point I decluttered sixty-seven pounds of rusty metal. Getting rid of that metal was getting rid of my dream of being a welder.

My father-in-law was a welder. Even though he was retired when my husband and I married, he had a workshop at his house full of welding tools, welding supplies, and the helmet thingies welders wear.

Yes, I totally called it a *helmet thingy*. Because knowing there are supplies required and some sort of special helmet that keeps you from burning your eyes completely out of your head is as far as I got on my personal welding journey.

At some point, early in my marriage, the easy access to welding equipment and an expert welding instructor was too much for my idea-loving brain to handle. How in the world could I possibly justify *not* learning to weld?

So I took the first (totally irrational in retrospect, but totally logical to me at the time) step: I headed to the junkyard.

Did you know that if you buy a bunch of scrap metal, you're supposed to have them weigh your vehicle first, and then load up the scrap metal, and then have them weigh your vehicle again so they can charge you by the difference between the two weights?

I didn't. So I did it wrong, and the junkyard guy (after a somewhat dramatic heavy-sigh) basically glanced at my pile of scrap metal and told me to give him three dollars.

Heading to the junkyard and collecting rebar, sheet metal, and such was as far as this hobby ever went. But still, I moved that load of random scrap metal four hours away when we moved, where it sat in our backyard and rusted.

Finally, I threw it away. I didn't even take it to a scrap yard to get my three dollars back.

I dream of doing cool things, of learning new skills, of being resourceful and crafty and interesting. And when opportunity collides with an idea, I can barely resist.

Once upon a time, I didn't even consider resisting. I *wanted* to bring sixty-seven pounds of metal into my home, because I never considered I might *not* one day be a welder.

This chapter is about decluttering dreams, but I'm dividing this subject into two parts: small dreams and big dreams.

Small dreams are things I wanted to do or be, but aren't life-altering if I don't get to do them or be them. Big dreams are life-altering.

SMALL DREAMS

Craft projects (or welding projects) you never finished are examples of small dreams. Small dreams can be hobbies that sounded great but didn't consume you the way you thought they would. They can be organizing solutions you were *sure* would work the way they did in the pictures, but totally did *not*.

While the two decluttering questions will take you through everything in your house, decluttering your dreams is nuanced.

Is This Actually a Dream?

Or is it a cool thing you thought you might like doing?

As a former garage sale addict/aficionado, I was always running across cool stuff. "Dreams" were often the result of an amazing price and me asking myself, *How could I say no?*

Those weren't dreams; they were opportunities.

I once bought two shopping bags full of stamps. Rubber stamps, wood stamps, and foam stamps. Someone spent money and time carefully collecting those stamps and then sold the entire collection to me for one dollar.

But I didn't stamp. I occasionally let my kids stamp gift bags for grandparents, but for those two or three incidents over two or three years, I stored sixty stamps in my cabinet. When I thought about letting them go, I felt like I was giving up on my dream (even though it was just a *cool thing*) of being the person who stamps.

Did You Inherit This Dream?

Is this your dream or someone else's?

Maybe Aunt Glenda was a quilter, and you inherited not only her beautiful creations but her supplies and fabric stash and quilt squares and a full-sized quilt stand.

An older neighbor once gave me a large box of glass bottles and etching supplies. She gave them to me because she knew I was creative. I accepted them gladly, but then they sat in my garage for years. I finally had to admit that etching glass is cool, but it isn't *my* dream.

Was Collecting the Stuff the Best Part of the Dream?

I dreamed of being (and assumed I would be) a baker. I watched baking shows and copied baking recipes. I gathered supplies and collected pans. But as real-life set in, I realized I wasn't capable of baking regularly. Mostly, I wasn't capable of *eating* baked goods regularly. And I didn't love baking quite as much as I'd assumed I would. But I struggled to declutter because of all the memories I had of collecting that stuff.

As Always, the Container Decides

Is this particular dream container worthy? Does this dream-related stuff deserve shelf space more than other, reality-related things in your home?

When I looked at my stuff that way, I was able to easily part with those bags of stamps. When I finally tackled the clutter in my kitchen, I had to admit I didn't have room for the baking stuff *and* the kitchen supplies I actually used.

> **Does this dream-related stuff deserve shelf space more than other, reality-related things in your home?**

Dreams that were only cool ideas were obvious when I understood limits—not limits to my dreams, but limits to the space available in my home.

But remember, start with easy stuff. Don't begin your decluttering journey by tackling dreams. Get rid of easy stuff. Purge things you don't like. Let your perspective change, learn how to declutter, and experience the impact decluttering has on your home so you can apply what you've learned to this difficult stuff.

Tips for Tackling Small-Dream Clutter

"Less" is a strangely effective decluttering mind-set change. Do you need *all* of the things you've collected for this dream, or could you survive with less? Having a few stamps was fun, but having two grocery sacks full of stamps was making life more difficult.

Even if you're not ready to purge everything related to this dream, look. I *have* to look. I can't assume I know what is inside a bag or a cabinet or how I'll feel about individual things in it. I'm always surprised to find things I don't even like or that are obviously trash, and when I get rid of the trash that was mixed in with my Dream Clutter, I sometimes find there's room in my container to keep it.

Do an identity reality check. So many of my small dreams were an identity issue. I had dreamed of being a certain person, and I collected things I thought that person would like to have. I was going to be the mom who threw herself into her family, who made home-cooked meals a reality. I intended to become a community leader who made people feel loved and special by doing things like making home-made cards. Homemade *stamped* cards.

My Dream Clutter represented how I thought my dreams would look once they were reality. I thought I was equipping Future Me at a bargain price, and I assumed gathering these things was wise.

Decluttering the things that represented the person I'd assumed I'd be was heart-aching because it made me question whether I was living up to the identity I had envisioned.

But I *did* achieve those identities. I cooked for my family. I invested in my community and focused on relationships, and I threw myself wholeheartedly into motherhood. The details of those identities just looked so different from how I'd assumed they'd look.

Being the mom who cooked for her family did not mean being the mom who spent hours in the kitchen, creating gourmet meals and milling her own flour. It meant shopping sales and pre-cooking meats in bulk so I could get a homemade meal on the table with minimal fuss and limited time.

Investing in my community didn't mean fancy dinner parties and homemade, handstamped greeting cards. It did mean taking an easy-to-freeze meal to a new mama or a friend who was starting chemo. It meant choreographing musicals for ten-year-old kids who needed to know there was more to life than baseball.

Throwing myself into my family meant wriggling into my bathing suit every single day of the Texas summer, and figuring out how to best use a Crock-Pot instead of a springform pan.

I'm all about living with intention, but living out that intention doesn't mean the details look exactly like I thought they might.

I didn't have an exact plan, but I collected things as they conveniently crossed my path, assuming Future Me would know exactly what to do with these things.

She was going to have it all together, of course.

I'm committed to living for now—for the situation and life stage I am in.

Break your paralysis by using your stuff. Stamp something. There's a chance you'll realize stamping is exactly what's been missing in your life for the past who-knows-how-long. But most likely, you'll see you only actually like three or four of the fifty stamps in your cabinet. You'll realize six out of seven ink pads are completely dry, and you don't like this hobby enough to pay full price for more ink.

And then decluttering will be easy. Yay for easy.

BIG DREAMS

Laughing about welding dreams is one thing, but what about dreams that aren't laughable?

What about dreams that cause tears to fall in the midst of random conversations?

Dreams of how you thought life would go or who you desperately wanted to be.

I got this question from a podcast listener:

I've been decluttering like crazy lately and donating a ton of my son's clothes, baby toys, etc., that I've been saving in hopes of having a second child. I'm now forty-seven, my son is eight, and

I'm finally accepting the reality that my dream is never going to happen. I'm pushing through with decluttering this stuff and also saving those truly special items, but it's been really emotional for me and I'm grieving. I guess the question is how to get through decluttering when it means you're facing reality and giving up on a dream (it would also be relevant to someone decluttering craft projects, workwear for a career that didn't work out, exercise equipment, items from a failed marriage, whatever).

I love that she acknowledges there are similarities between small dreams and the huge life dreams she's letting go.

They boil down to this: *I thought one day I would _____, but now I've realized I never will.*

Big and small dreams are completely different, though, in regard to who is in control. I could have welded. I had everything I needed to weld. I just didn't. The pain I feel about giving up on welding is regret.

The pain she feels as she realizes she will not have more children is grief. Grief and regret are different things.

Big dreams that require decluttering usually also require grief.

Require it. Grief is a thing. It happens whether you're planning for it or not. Some people manage to go their entire lives without bringing home a minivan full of things they don't actually need, but no one avoids the pain of life not going exactly as he or she planned.

But sometimes you don't realize that what you're going through is grief.

When I was a newlywed, a friend shared a great perspective. There's a form of grief that's common in new marriages. As you work to build the so-called perfect relationship, putting time and energy and focus on what it means to do marriage right, you start seeing the flaws in your own childhood and family. While the way your family functioned was normal to you because it was all you knew, working on your own marriage means identifying things you want to do differently.

Strangely, there's grief in that. Grief over having grown up in an environment that wasn't as ideal as you'd always assumed it was. Grief over having that veil lifted, over changed memories.

This isn't a chapter about marriage, but that conversation opened up a new way of thinking for me. I realized grief is more than intense sadness and can be present at times when you don't even realize you're grieving. Grieving is the process of emotionally navigating a loss. Navigating the loss of a dream is where grief can come as a surprise.

It's possible to grieve something you never had. This is what so many people grieving the loss of a loved one are experiencing. The loss of a loved one's presence is devastating, but grief returns in waves as time brings reminders of things that should have happened for that one who is gone. A parent who loses a child also loses the opportunity to visit colleges with that child. A wife who loses her husband loses the partner who was supposed to be there to help make daunting decisions.

And that's what is important to understand about grief: There are stages, and walking through those stages isn't only important, it's necessary. And unfortunately, unavoidable.

Prince Harry of England was interviewed in 2017 on *Bryony Gordon's Mad World* podcast. He shared that at the age of twenty-eight he finally faced his grief over his mother's death, sixteen years after she'd been gone. For years he thought he could avoid grief, but he couldn't. He had to walk through it.

There isn't any way to get around grief. There's only walking through, and even then it's not about coming out on the other side unscathed. It's about coming out a changed person.

The stages of grief are real. Knowing what the phases are doesn't prevent hurt, and getting through them doesn't mean you forget. But understanding that the phases are legitimate and identifying your own stage in the process can help you feel a little less crazy.

A lot of my own clutter is directly linked to denial. I have to fight against living in denial. If something is unpleasant or stressful, I'll purposely deny it. Ignore it. If I think an e-mail is going to say something I don't want to hear, I put off opening it.

But with grief, denial is a phase.

It's a legitimate stop on the Grief Walk Trail, and there's no alternate path to walk around it.

I have had closets full of denial—denial that my teaching career was over. That the games and ideas and quizzes I worked so hard to create are truly of no use to me now.

I've tripped over boxes full of denial—denial that I really might never get my master's degree. That my life had really taken a completely different direction.

So what's the easiest way to get through denial? (Not around, not over, but through?)

Noncommittal Decluttering

Touch things. I've said it again and again. Look. Always, always look. Assuming what is in a box or at the back of a shelf does no good whatsoever.

But assuming is the hardest thing for me to fight in my war against clutter. I see a mass of stuff and assume it's full of emotions. I assume every last item in the pile, box, or closet will rip my heart right out of my chest.

Every single item will represent a part of life I'm not ready to accept is over.

If you're fighting denial, give yourself permission to go through your things and *not even declutter*. Today is the day for letting yourself feel. For touching things, even if not one item goes into the trash bag or the Donate Box.

There's a chance you'll be surprised that the box or cabinet contains things with no emotional value alongside things that are packed with emotions. If you've followed my advice and have already decluttered nonemotional stuff, you will likely be surprised at the effects of the decluttering experience you've gained.

But tricking yourself into decluttering is not the point. The point is to just touch the things. Feel the feelings. Remember these things you're keeping out of fear you'll forget.

Don't wear mascara. Go for it with zero expectations.

And then, let yourself live awhile.

If I make myself look at or read through something I don't want to look at or read through, my brain does strange things after I'm done. When I go back again to that space, whether it's been a year or a month, I generally have a shifted perspective on the stuff that was so difficult last time.

I am not a grief counselor, and I don't pretend to understand the intensity of your loss. But if there is a physical representation of that grief, physically holding those items is a way to purposefully walk through the pain. I know from general clutter experience that avoiding doesn't work.

There's No Perfect Way

Do what you want to do. If you feel the need to (legally) burn boxes without looking inside, go for it (after you check local burn laws). There's no right way to declutter.

Or keep what you are desperate to keep. But acknowledge that the Container Concept is fact. If you truly can't part with these dreams, what *are* you willing to part with so you can keep them?

Maybe the box full of outgrown Halloween costumes is easy to let go once you realize you need that shelf space for the business suits you can't bear to donate. Maybe maternity clothes can go in the spot where you've kept that box of hand-me-downs you hated so your kid never wore.

Or maybe viewing the closet shelf as a container helps you realize you're not willing to let your fear of letting go of tailored jackets keep you from being the mom who can outfit every neighborhood kid as a superhero at the same time. Maybe you're ready to embrace that mom identity and let go of your professional identity.

Decluttering is about identifying the stuff you really want to keep, in a way that you can handle.

Is this stuff making the life you have *harder* to live? Are you giving priority to things that never happened over the things that are happening now?

There's more to your grief than your clutter. Seeing a therapist is what people determined to be emotionally healthy do. Find one in your area, or join a grief support group.

Tips for Tackling Big-Dream Clutter

Now that we've spent some time on the touchy-feely side of big, heart-ripping dreams, let's deal with the practical side. I'm going to use the office wardrobe as an example. Please know I am aware your unique dream-clutter issue may be completely different and much more significant than an office wardrobe. But if an office wardrobe is your unique issue, also know that I understand how much that wardrobe once represented your identity and how difficult giving up that identity, either voluntarily or by force, can be.

Is it truly sentimental, or is it a what-if scenario? The money and time spent to collect an expensive office wardrobe can be a legitimate reason to want to hold on to it. But how legitimate is that fear in reality? Are these classic pieces, or are they part of a trend that will be over before you might need them again?

Can you reduce? Keep one or some? If you've purged easy stuff like the tops with underarm discoloration (from the high-stress meetings you used to have), stains, or tears, is it still possible to reduce some more? Can you reduce the stock to one or two pairs of black pants instead of the ten you once justified having? Can you keep the three power suits you wore more than anything else?

Consolidate. As you've identified Dream Clutter you truly can't purge, consolidate. Put all of your office wear together instead of letting it mix with other clothes in your closet.

Physically putting things together is key for my own reality check in my home. I grasp the actual volume of an item I have. So many times, seeing all of it together wakes me up to how much of my home a certain dream is taking up, and that frees me to see it for what it is: clutter.

If office suits were mixed in with yoga pants and college sweatshirts, I would have no idea how much space is being given to office suits.

Physically touching things makes me acknowledge them. Do I, no longer a theatre teacher, need to keep my costume stash? Maybe not. But I did. When I put the costumes all together, I touched each item before I put it in the container. This helped me get rid of a lot of things I couldn't justify putting in the designated space I had. It also freed other spaces in my home for other things. And if I do need costumes, I can find them more easily. They're together, in a spot for costumes.

DON'T START HERE

Dreams are difficult to declutter. Don't start with dreams. Get rid of easy stuff first. Decluttering momentum is real, and the worst place to start is with the stuff that makes your heart hurt. Don't start with the stuff that makes you feel like you're donating a piece of your soul.

Throw away trash. Get rid of stuff you hate. Clear visible spaces of stuff that has an established, nonemotional place elsewhere in the home. Focus on neutral stuff.

One of two things will happen: You'll end up with space to give these dreams a home and yourself room to live well. Or your perspective will change as you begin valuing space over stuff—and living now instead of in the past or the future—and this Dream Clutter will look very different to you by the time you tackle it. Either way, your house will be better off.

The hardest part of giving yourself permission to walk through the stages of grief is knowing that you will come through the stages different than you are now. Change will happen. You will change. And change is scary.

But changing doesn't mean forgetting, ignoring, or even giving up. You are ready for change because you're ready for your house to change. That's why you are reading this book.

Chapter 26

A LIFESTYLE OF DECLUTTERING

Ultimately, decluttering at the speed of life is a matter of living a lifestyle of decluttering. Acknowledge that decluttering is a constant task and will be a constant task for the rest of your life. (Sorry.)

The good news is that decluttering as a lifestyle won't be overwhelming like it was this first time. The key to preventing the reappearance of overwhelming piles and closets full of stuff is to acknowledge that decluttering needs to be part of your everyday life. And then make it part of your everyday life.

START THE BIG PURGE TODAY

The only real way to change your view of clutter is to declutter. The only way to break through that paralyzing feeling of being overwhelmed is to declutter. The only way to not be intimidated by the boxes and piles and closets full of stuff is to declutter. And now you know exactly where to start. Grab a trash bag and throw away trash.

Decluttering isn't a once-and-for-all task, but it *is* a task that gets easier every time. And unlike floors that get muddy and dishes that get dirty, once something leaves your home, it's gone. You'll never need to declutter that item again.

PRIORITIZE BY VISIBILITY

Do not underestimate the need to prioritize according to visibility. Every single time you work on your home, follow the Visibility Rule. This will build momentum, will increase your own energy, and will go further in creating a lifestyle of decluttering than anything else.

STOP THE INFLUX

As you declutter, your view of stuff will change. Use that change to help you identify clutter *before* it turns into clutter. See the papers or the souvenir cups or even the super useful reusable binder as the future clutter it is. The physical act of purging clutter will cause alarm bells to go off in your head and the foggy haze to clear as you see the future of the item in your hand and put it down before it ever enters your home.

As new stuff does enter your home (because it will), let it replace things that are already there. As a new set of dishes gets put away, place the old dishes in a Donate Box. When you purchase a new jacket, get rid of an old one. Replacing instead of adding allows you to continue to live under the Clutter Threshold you've discovered. Replacing old things as new things come in is the key to maintaining any decluttering progress you make.

LIVE—RIGHT NOW—IN YOUR OWN HOME

As you throw away trash and start with the easy stuff, view every space in your home according to your present. Plan for the future and acknowledge the past, but live now. Commit to creating a home that makes living now fun.

ESTABLISH A DONATE SPOT

A Donate Spot is essential to living a lifestyle of decluttering. It is the designated place where the entire family knows to take something if we realize we no longer need it.

Having a Donate Spot means that in the moment I realize I don't like that skillet, or in the moment my son realizes his pants are too short, I (and my family members) know exactly what to do. We head for the Donate Box, which is in the Donate Spot.

And the more that happens, the more decluttering isn't a big dramatic thing. The more likely I am to realize and admit that if I don't want to wear this itchy sweater today, I'm not going to want to wear it tomorrow or next year.

FIVE-MINUTE PICKUPS

Unfortunately, daily habits are the key to maintaining progress. Sorry. But the good news (as I explained in exhaustive detail in *How to Manage Your Home Without Losing Your Mind*) is that decluttering makes those habits easier.

The habit that will prevent the mysterious reappearance of clutter and will truly allow you to declutter at the speed of life is the five-minute pickup. Set your timer for five minutes and pick up. Use the take-it-there-right-now strategy and spend five minutes a day (or almost every day) putting things away.

Those five minutes matter. They are the difference between a decluttered kitchen counter that gets increasingly re-cluttered, and a clear kitchen counter staying clear.

You know all about the Clutter Creep, right? How you look up one day while still thinking you've decluttered "not that long ago" and suddenly see the clutter has re-appeared? The five-minute pickup is the difference between that happening and that not happening. Try it. You'll be shocked at the impact.

HAVING LESS STUFF MAKES IT MUCH EASIER TO CLEAN

I understand the fear that you will run out of clean dishes or clean socks if you get rid of any. But cleaning is easier when you have less stuff. Even if you do run out of socks or coffee cups, washing them will be approximately 1,643 times easier, faster, and less overwhelming than when you used to run out of coffee cups.

And big-time cleaning like scrubbing bathrooms and mopping kitchens can't even compare. If you dream of a home where you could just scrub or just mop without first spending an hour (or more) clearing the surfaces you need to scrub and mop, declutter.

USE YOUR CALENDAR

I'm guessing you've laughed (or lamented) that the best way to make yourself declutter is to invite someone over. You were right. Nothing opens my eyes to otherwise invisible clutter like knowing someone other than us will see it.

Invite some friends over for a game night. Start hosting a book club. Suggest switching off babysitting every other week with a friend who has kids the same ages as yours. I know the thought of doing these things is overwhelming, but as you begin doing the easy stuff, let your visible progress inspire you to pick up the phone.

Just a few weeks into my own deslobification process, I raised my trembling hand to volunteer to host a weekly group in my own home. My husband looked at me like I had lost my mind. But having a weekly deadline to re-clear the spaces I was decluttering was one of the best things I ever did for my home.

DO THE EASY STUFF

I desperately hope that as you finish this book, you feel both empowered and inspired to start on your decluttering journey. I know the temptation to start by renting a Dumpster. Don't. Just grab a trash bag. If you don't have a black one, use whatever you have. Today, throw away trash. Do the easy stuff first, and you'll be on your way to decluttering at the speed of life.

ACKNOWLEDGMENTS

Thank you, Bob, for your encouragement and support as I wrote this book and for putting up with all the trial and error I went through to learn the things that are in it. Thanks for letting our home be the setting for all my crazy experiments. Thanks for supporting the book-writing journey both emotionally and practically and for volunteering to take over cooking while I met this insane deadline. You are my favorite person.

Jackson, Reid, and Presley, thank you for still being supportive of what I do, even though you're old enough now to understand the irony of the fact that I write about cleaning and organizing even though/because I struggle with it more than your friends' moms do.

Thank you, Linda and Hali and Maryann, for helping me keep the blog going while my tunnel vision flared as I wrote this book.

Thank you, Mom and Dad, for parenting in a way that gave me the confidence to stand up and speak for those who struggle in this area, many of whom weren't given the gift of unconditional acceptance that you gave me.

Thank you to my agent, Jessica Kirkland, and to all the people at Thomas Nelson who understand the message and are excited to help spread it.

Thank you, Doug the Housekeeper, for leaving a comment on the blog years ago that opened my eyes to the fact that my favorite stuff was the stuff outside the cabinets. You're smart!

Acknowledgments

Thank you, Stephanie McNeilly, for reconnecting fifteen years after we shared a classroom in our first year as teachers, and for saying "Sure!" when I sent you the draft just days before it was due. Your insights and honesty had such a big impact on the book.

Thank you to Jen L., for answering the question I asked about specific struggles people wanted me to address in the second book with the words, "I have trouble decluttering at the speed of life." You inspired the title of this book.

ABOUT THE AUTHOR

DANA K. WHITE is a blogger, speaker, and (much to her own surprise) Decluttering Expert. She taught both English and theatre arts before leaving her job to make her family her life's work. In an attempt to get her home under control, Dana started blogging as Nony (short for Anonymous) at *A Slob Comes Clean*. She soon realized she was not alone in her housekeeping struggles and in her feelings of shame. Today, Dana shares realistic home management strategies and a message of hope for the hopelessly messy through her blog, weekly podcasts, and videos. Dana lives with her husband and three kids just outside of Dallas, Texas. Oh, and she's funny.

Connect with Dana and join a community of people who are learning to declutter at the speed of life at http://www .aslobcomesclean.com/speed

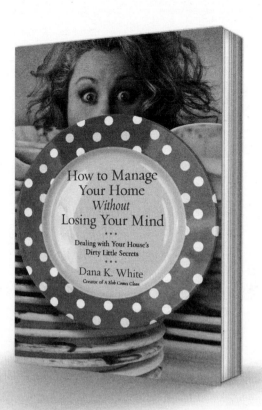

ALSO AVAILABLE FROM DANA K. WHITE

Bring your home out of the mess it's in and learn how to keep it under control!

Cleaning your house is not a onetime project but a series of ongoing premade decisions. Discover reality-based cleaning and organizing techniques that debunk the biggest housekeeping fantasies and create lasting change in your home.

Available wherever books and ebooks are sold.